CHARACTER EDUCATION

Grades 6–12
Year 2

by John Heidel and
Marion Lyman-Mersereau

Incentive Publications, Inc.
Nashville, Tennessee

Acknowledgments

We would like to acknowledge the many people who supported us in this project. We are indebted to these people who have given of their time and energy to help bring this project to completion.

First, we would like to name the Character Education Committee of Punahou School which conceived of the idea for this project. They set us on the right path with suggestions for what they need, as teachers, to better help in the intentional character education of our students. Special thanks to the Review Committee who offered encouragement and thoughtfully critiqued our work.

In addition, we would like to thank the many other people who provided their time and expertise in developing this complete Character Education program.

Illustrated by Marta Drayton
Cover by Bill Latta
Edited by Jennifer E. Janke

Library of Congress Catalog Card Number: 98-75493
ISBN 0-86530-430-0

PRINTED IN THE UNITED STATES OF AMERICA

TABLE OF CONTENTS

INTRODUCTION

Twenty-five hundred years ago, Socrates defined education as helping students gain both knowledge and virtue, to become both smart and good. In recent decades schools sometimes consciously and sometimes unconsciously have lost their focus on this historic mission. Now, however, educators are being called back to help children gain the virtues, the embedded habits, which constitute good character. Often those calling for character education are parents. Increasingly, they are politicians articulating the will of worried citizens. A few scholars have recognized the current lack in our schools and have become champions for character education. While these voices have been articulate in pointing out the problems of a value-neutral school or a school that rejects responsibility for character formation, these voices are limited. They lack the knowledge of and experience with the instructional issues surrounding this topic. They do not speak to the real world of schools. The authors of this book possess that knowledge and experience.

John Heidel and Marion Lyman-Mersereau have written a book that takes character education to a new level, a level that enables teachers and administrators to go beyond the abstract into that real world of their classrooms and their schools. *Character Education* is based on the authors' action research project at one of the truly lighthouse schools of our nation, the Punahou School in Hawaii.

The book reflects a complete plan for engaging a school community in the mission of character development. Central to their work and to the organization of the book is a school-wide, monthly focus on a particular virtue, such as respect or courage. In this, they are addressing one of the core problems with school's efforts to respond to the call for character education. Americans, and particularly American educators, have frequently replaced the language of moral values and virtue with the language of psychology. Cheating is referred to as "inappropriate behavior" rather than "wrong." The goal has been "student development" and "adjustment," but development *into what* and adjustment *to what* has been left vague or unstated. This book and the program it offers educators, while on the one hand being new and fresh, returns us to an older, richer language system, one based on views of human excellence.

Over a two-year cycle, students are introduced to a deeper meaning of common words, such as loyalty, commitment and wisdom. It is here that the authors' gifts as educators become apparent. Students are not simply told the meaning of these virtue words. They are immersed in them. During the months that a particular word is being studied, each day there is a new activity which will give them greater experience and thus deeper understanding of the concept behind the word. Activities range from journal writing to a structured conversation with parents, from creating a poster about the virtue to listing ways students can practice the virtue in their everyday lives.

One of the most plaguing problems of American education is the continuing search for "the one right way": the one right way to teach reading, the one right way to evaluate student performance, the one right way to discipline students. As character education is again becoming a concern of educators, this same one-right-way mentality is becoming evident. The authors of *Character Education* take a very different approach, one that recognizes that children have very different ways of learning and that the best way to master something is to acquire it in several different learning modes. Therefore, the book offers students and teachers a rich reservoir of stories, sayings, and biographical sketches, which together bring out the depth of these concepts and show how they exist in a human life.

Character formation has been described as what we do to help students *know the good, love the good,* and *do the good.* This book addresses all dimensions of that description. The great power and benefit of *Character Education* is its appeal to the student's head, heart, and hands.

Kevin Ryan
Director of the Center for the Advancement of Ethics and Character,
Boston University

PURPOSE

Since one of the primary concerns of this program specifically relates to the total development of students, it is important to remember what a complete student is. A complete student is one who succeeds academically, but also portrays a strong moral character, with a clear sense of right and wrong.

It is probably a good exercise to reflect on how educators are doing. Most people would agree that schools across the country are doing well with academic goals and not so well with character goals. We have many students who don't know how to properly love themselves or each other, or who cheat on their schoolwork. There is teasing, gossiping, inappropriate language, and stealing. There are problems with litter and a general lack of common courtesy and good manners. We have a lot of work to do before we can fulfill the dream of a nation filled with complete students.

Thomas Lickona, developmental psychologist and author of *Educating for Character*, asserts that " . . . character must be broadly conceived to encompass the cognitive, affective, and behavioral aspects of morality. Good character consists of knowing the good, loving the good, and doing the good. Schools must help children understand the core values, adopt or commit to them, and then act upon them in their own lives."

While it might be difficult to teach values, the educational process at least can make known to students certain universal values. Students can be motivated and inspired to incorporate these values into their lives. The final step of acting out these values can be taken by giving students opportunity for community service and showing them how these values can be acted out in the community, on the playground, in the cafeteria, and in the classroom.

The purpose of this program is to design a structure whereby teachers can be more focused and intentional in their efforts to provide character education. Teachers should keep in touch with each other about activities that work, and design ways to involve parents and the wider community so the values will be reinforced. Teachers need to be conscious of who they are as role models and what values are reflected by their actions.

In all ways, our purpose is to assist teachers in their efforts to create a classroom environment where students can grow socially and spiritually, as well as intellectually. If these ideas prove useful we will be very gratified. We acknowledge the right of teachers to make this choice and to decide on their level of involvement. We know teachers enjoy autonomy, so there is room for flexibility and the development of personal style.

Much has been written about the present moral environment from which our children and youth choose their values. We know about the decline of the family, the lack of good adult models, the pervasive influence of the media, the problems of public schools, and the troubling trends in youth character. Another reason for this changing scene of morality can be traced through the gradual shift in the operative values that have characterized American life. Since the arrival of the Puritans and their lifestyle of honesty, faith, and hard work, there has been a big change. Sociologist Max Lerner made a study of American values in the mid-1950s and published his findings in *America As A Civilization* in 1957. He maintains that the idealistic values of early America became contaminated by money, materialism, competition, and success. "By the turn of the twentieth century a new pattern of life purposes emerged. Its components were success, prestige, money, power, and security." This "five-goal system" seemed to characterize the basic drives and behavioral patterns of most Americans. These five questionable values are alive and well today.

We are hopeful this program will offer other choices and have a positive impact on the daily life within each classroom and with relationships outside the classroom. This is the primary step that educators can take in reordering the moral environment of America with universal values that affirm life and enhance everyone's health and happiness. We can play an important role in the process of restoring a sense of what is right and good for our common life as Americans.

VALUE OF THE MONTH

The framework around which this project is designed is the idea of emphasizing a specific value each month. We chose eighteen values to be the featured values over a two year cycle and 36 others as supportive values. We decided on eighteen because that would give us a two-year cycle of nine values a year. This way we won't be repeating the same values each year and, with a different focus in each grade level, the values should stay fresh.

There is a specific reason for beginning with respect, following with responsibility, and leading toward compassion, faith, and commitment. It will be explained how one leads to the next and how each remains connected to all of the previous values. Some relate to seasonal themes and others become part of a total picture. However, this format is completely flexible and educators may develop their own schedule if students or current events warrant it.

VALUE OF THE MONTH BY TWO-YEAR CYCLE

In the first year students studied:

September	**Respect**	*Acceptance*	*Kindness*
October	**Responsibility**	*Self-discipline*	*Reliability*
November	**Compassion**	*Service*	*Generosity*
December	**Faith**	*Hope*	*Trust*
January	**Commitment**	*Loyalty*	*Effort*
February	**Love**	*Friendship*	*Sincerity*
March	**Wisdom**	*Knowledge*	*Understanding*
April	**Health**	*Holistic Living*	*Serenity*
May	**Humor**	*Joy*	*Enthusiasm*

In the second year, students expand their character development by learning about:

September	**Honesty**	*Integrity*	*Truth*
October	**Cooperation**	*Family*	*Unity*
November	**Humility**	*Gratitude*	*Appreciation*
December	**Peace**	*Harmony*	*Forgiveness*
January	**Patience**	*Perseverance*	*Confidence*
February	**Courage**	*Tenacity*	*Conviction*
March	**Creativity**	*Wonder*	*Resourcefulness*
April	**Environmental Awareness**	*Beauty*	*Sacrifice*
May	**Freedom**	*Social Justice*	*Equality*

LEVELS OF FACULTY INVOLVEMENT

Basic

Aware of how busy teachers are and how much is already asked, the basic involvement is quite simple. Yet, if we accept this project as important, there is great value in everyone's involvement. A clear message of the school's intention will be sent to the students and to the wider community. Hopefully, there will be a general feeling of cohesion as teachers share stories about what works and as students talk about each value from their own experience.

Therefore, basic involvement would mean supporting and following the value-of-the-month idea. Specifically, it would mean posting a sign bearing the current month's value, making the students aware of it, finding a connection with your curriculum once a week, and citing an example of someone acting out that value once a week; preferably "catching a student," but also examples from the community and the world. You can take this as far as your time and interest allow, from a short announcement to a discussion.

A Little Extra

You may want to do a little extra for any of the following reasons: the value of the month goes well with your subject area or curriculum, it relates to a current event or issue within the school or worldwide, it reflects one of your concerns, or you just want to explore the possibilities a little more.

In that case, use the extensive information provided on each value in this handbook. There will be suggested activities and, where appropriate, material that will deal with specific issues such as inappropriate language, cheating, or stealing. These activities will include stories, quotations, material from world religions, biographies of heroes and heroines, values in other languages, discussion questions, and community service ideas. Another suggestion is to follow up a school assembly presentation with a discussion or writing assignment. This level of involvement would mean utilizing these resources two or three times a month.

Beyond the Call

Some people may become so excited about the possibilities of this program that they will use many or all of the suggested calendar of activities. In that case, go for it!

Calendar

At the beginning of each month there is a calendar of suggested activities outlining a lesson plan for that month. No matter the level of involvement chosen, this calendar should help educators fit *Character Education* into their monthly routine. These calendars show daily activities which focus on the value of that month. The calendar can be used to help educators develop creative ways to teach *Character Education*. The schedule need not be followed exactly—this is only one example of how a *Character Education* lesson plan might look.

COMMENTS FROM TEACHERS

- The character education program has given us a focus each month, and points of reference to remember during the entire school year. When problems arise in class, we often discuss the various values . . .

- In the past we have incorporated character-building and values education in our daily teaching; the curriculum project . . . certainly helped us to include these topics with our classroom activities in a more organized way . . .

- The Values of the Month that were put together . . . were a tremendous asset to the school.

- I would like to extend my appreciation . . . for the Character Education program which has set the tone to this year . . .

- I am so pleased that Punahou has included values as an integral part of our curriculum. As an educator, there is no way I would downplay knowledge; yet as a parent and concerned adult I believe that to be truly enlightened, a person must possess clear and honorable values and a moral character.

- I can't help but feel that our focus on values has brought about a positive change in our day-to-day goings-on. Good mornings and pleases and thank-yous abounded . . .

- The Character Education Handbook filled with guidelines and ideas for the incorporation of given values into the daily curriculum is one of the most significant steps that has taken place at Punahou . . . It resets a standard that speaks to the community at large about Punahou's stand regarding the necessity of spiritual values in daily living.

- I felt the character education program was a great success. Having the quotes in the daily bulletin and the signs in the classroom, cafeteria—everywhere—was very effective; it kept those values in the forefront of our day . . . [it] made us realize that these values were not just something to "teach" our kids, but they were ideals to be sought after by every adult on campus. In a sense they unified us . . . the signs/values provided me and my students with a common language for our discussions of themes in our literature.

- The addition and recognition of character education as an integral part of the total curriculum of the school has been long awaited and fully embraced by all students, parents, faculty, staff and administrators alike.

- Start at the kindergarten level and continue through academy years, if not already doing so. There cannot be too much character development!

* *These comments were unsolicited and were written after the first year of the program as piloted at Punahou School.*

PARENTAL AND COMMUNITY INVOLVEMENT

The statement, "It takes a whole village to raise a child" refers to the community of support necessary for the upbringing of students. We acknowledge that this is not a task that we educators do alone. Much of a school's success is a result of parental involvement. Parental support in reinforcing a school's educational goals for their children is imperative. We, therefore, feel it is important for parents to be aware of this particular program so that they may more actively participate in reinforcing these goals of Character Education.

Through announcements, newsletters, and various other methods of communication, educators can keep parents informed of the Value of the Month, related activities, and opportunities to attend workshops or selected speaker engagements.

Our dreams for Character Education go beyond the triangle of parents, teachers, and students to include the community outside of school. As Thomas Lickona writes, the long term success of any values education depends on " . . . the extent to which families and communities join schools in a common effort to meet the needs of children and foster their healthy development."

Here are some excerpts from letters of support our project has received from parents and the community around our school:

> *I am writing to applaud and commend you for attacking what I think is at the very heart of a world wide epidemic . . . During the next 1½ years, I will encourage physicians to focus on the importance of personal responsibility and other attributes of character building. I will encourage physicians to assist in spreading this message via the media and to address the community with appropriate speeches.*
> — Carl W. Lehman, M. D.
> President, Hawaii Medical Association .

> *While I do teach at a Buddhist-affiliated school, the general philosophy and the values on which the Character Education program is based are universal. I will be sharing the program with all Middle School teachers and the Reverends who instruct the students in religious education.*
> — Lynette Araki
> Hongwanji Mission School

> *The Character Education program . . . is a breath of fresh air, and I encourage you . . . to vigorously continue this initiative for the sake of our children, our community, and our country.*
> — M. G. MacLaren

> *Your "village" concept has led me to conclude that we probably have more villages than we realize . . . , and, more importantly, that those villages don't communicate with each other very well. That is probably our ultimate challenge before we can really solve some of the underlying issues.*
> — Ed Case
> Representative, 23rd District, Hawaii

SUGGESTED LETTER TO PARENTS

Dear 6–12 Parents,

As we begin the second year of our *Character Education*, we continue to encourage parental and community involvement in the hope that we can make an integrated effort to influence our students' positive character development from as many directions as possible. We will continue our work inside and outside the classroom to develop the character of our students.

Mark Twain's quip, "To be good is noble, to teach others to be good is nobler—and less trouble," speaks to our work in character education and is reminiscent of G. B. Shaw's often heard droll remark, "Those who can, do . . . " Kurt Hahn, the father of Outward Bound, wilderness schools of experiential education, offers the following suggestion for teachers, which is more helpful than Twain and Shaw, when we think about Character Education:

> *There are three ways of trying to win the young. There is persuasion, there is compulsion, and there is attraction. You can preach at them, that is a hook without a worm; you can say, "You must volunteer," that is [compulsion]; and you can tell them, "You are needed," that appeal hardly ever fails.*

Once again the program will emphasize a value of the month with two partner values. This year's values for each month are:

September	**Honesty**, Integrity, Truth
October	**Cooperation**, Family, Unity
November	**Humility**, Gratitude, Appreciation
December	**Peace**, Harmony, Forgiveness
January	**Patience**, Perseverance, Confidence
February	**Courage**, Tenacity, Conviction
March	**Creativity**, Wonder, Resourcefulness
April	**Environmental Awareness**, Beauty, Sacrifice
May	**Freedom**, Social Justice, Equality

We look forward to continuing to work with you on this joint effort of providing a complete education for your children.

Sincerely,

Honesty

SUPPORTIVE VALUES

Integrity • Truth

DEFINITIONS

Telling the truth; straightforward conduct.

The definition for **honesty** goes beyond being truthful in speech, it also assumes a way of conducting oneself. Shakespeare's classic and timeless piece of advice in *Hamlet* from Polonius to his son probably best describes the partnership of honesty and behavior toward others: "To thine own self be true, And it must follow, as the night the day, Thou canst not then be false to any man."

Integrity is the firm adherence to a moral code. Integrity is the state of being complete or undivided. Synonyms for integrity are incorruptibility and completeness and the antonym which furthers our understanding of the word is duplicity.

Truth is sincerity in action, character, and speech. When we examine the word further we see it is often capitalized and refers to a spiritual reality. In some spiritual traditions, Truth is synonymous with God.

PURPOSE

In a school faculty survey, honesty came up third in number of votes, after respect and responsibility, as the most important value for students to learn. It is obvious that teachers are concerned about the prevalence of cheating on schoolwork and tests and the "but everybody else does it" attitude which accompanies this behavior. The win-at-all-costs, dog-eat-dog ethic appears to be entrenched among many students. The importance placed on achievement and the rewards and recognition which accompany the accomplishment has clearly undermined the value of honesty. We somehow need to express our indignation at dishonest conduct and communicate how much we esteem honest actions. Honor codes in the classrooms and sportsmanship in athletics, demonstrated by calling fouls on oneself, would affirm expectations we have for appreciating and valuing honesty.

September

Honesty

Day One:
Discuss the meaning of honesty. As references, use the definitions on page 17.

Day Two:
If you discover someone has lied to you—how does that make you feel? Make a list of words which describe your feelings. Does it matter what that person lied about? Why or why not?

Day Three:
As best you can, pronounce the foreign words on page 19. Discuss the cultures of the countries represented.

Day Four:
In a total class setting, create a list of categories of people whom you expect to be honest. (A few to get you started are: family, government officials, law enforcement officers, and teachers.)

Day Five:
Why is it sometimes difficult to be honest? Why should you be honest even when it may get you in trouble? Select a bookmark on page 27 to keep in your desk to remind you to be honest even when it might be uncomfortable to do so.

Day Six:
Discuss cheating. Why is cheating being dishonest? How would it feel if someone cheated on you? What would you say to that person to explain how you feel?

Day Seven:
When in court, a witness must promise to tell "the truth, the whole truth, and nothing but the truth"—what does that phrase mean to you?

Day Eight:
How does a person's *honor* relate to his or her *honesty*? Look up the words in a dictionary if you need help to compare and contrast their meanings. Is it possible to be honorable without being honest?

Day Nine:
To be honest requires a commitment. Write yourself a letter of encouragement to be honest. Save the letter to refer to later as a "self-reminder" to be honest.

Day Ten:
Why are good relationships dependent on honesty? How would you feel about a person you enjoy being with, but whom you found to be constantly lying to you?

Day Eleven:
Select a story about honesty from pages 21–26. Read and discuss the story's message about honesty.

Day Twelve:
Plagiarism is a form of being dishonest. Do you understand why? Look up the definition of plagiarism and discuss how to avoid it in your own schoolwork and recognize it in the work of others.

Day Thirteen:
What is "the truth"? How do you know when someone is telling you the truth? Write about it in your journal.

Day Fourteen:
Why is it important to be honest with yourself. What does being honest with yourself mean to how you live your life. Write a journal entry to organize your thoughts on "self-honesty."

Day Fifteen:
Why is honesty an important value to embrace throughout your life? What are the benefits? Work in small groups to brainstorm a list to share with the entire class.

Day Sixteen:
Review the letter you wrote to yourself about honesty. Have you remembered to be honest in all things at all times?

Day Seventeen:
Read about the heroes and heroines of honesty on pages 28–29. What can we learn about how to be honest from the actions of these people?

Day Eighteen:
Why did Abraham Lincoln develop the name "Honest Abe"? Do some research. Share the story with a younger person to demonstrate the value of honesty.

Day Nineteen:
Write a thank you letter to a person whom you feel has always been honest with you.

Day Twenty:
Reflect on the lessons about honesty that you have learned this month and think about specific steps that you can take right now to begin to embrace honesty as a lifetime value.

HONESTY IN OTHER LANGUAGES

Chinese	*cheng* *shi*	sincere; true; honest; to make sincere solid; substantial; hard; real; true
French	*l'honnêteté*	characteristic of a person or of behavior which shows conformity to rules of morality, probity or loyalty
German	*ehrlichkeit*	honesty, honorable dealing, fairness
Hawaiian	*kupono*	upright, honest (ku means "to stand" and pono means "goodness, uprightness, morality")
Japanese	*makoto*	to make what you say happen or to do what you say
Korean	*jin shil*	right and straight; integrity
Latin	*probitas*	from Latin "honestus" (honorable); from "honos" (honor) (something that is held in honor)
Spanish	*honradez*	honesty, integrity, uprightness
Tagalog	*katapatan*	fair, upright and just in all aspects of personal behavior

Character Education Year 2 Grades 6–12

DISCUSSION QUESTIONS

- Why is it difficult to maintain a friendship with someone who doesn't tell the truth?

- What is a "white lie?" Why is it potentially harmful?

- Why is it wrong to cheat on your homework or on a test?

- Why do people cheat? Does it lead to other kinds of dishonesty?

- Would you be brave enough to express your disagreement with someone who is dishonest? Give an example.

- Why is it important to be honest with oneself?

- Do you agree with this statement: "The test of genuine honesty is how you act when no one is looking." How does this relate to cheating?

- Would you question your parents' effort to buy you a child's ticket at the movies? What would you say?

- What is the difference between stating the truth "as you see it" and being tactful? Can you be honest and tactful at the same time? Give an example.

- Would you call a foul on yourself in whatever sport you play, both in practice and in games? Why is this important?

- Why is there so much dishonesty in our society (politics, business, and personal)?

STORIES AND THOUGHTS FROM SPIRITUAL TRADITIONS

Hinduism

The Lord is the one life shining forth from every creature. Seeing him present in all, the wise man is humble, puts not himself forward. His delight is in the Self, his joy is in the Self, he serves the Lord in all. Such as he, indeed, are the true knowers of Brahman.

This Effulgent Self is to be realized within the lotus of the heart by continence, by steadfastness in truth, by meditation, and by superconscious vision. Their impurities washed away, the seers realize him.

Truth alone succeeds, not untruth. By truthfulness the path of felicity is opened up, the path which is taken by the sages, freed from cravings, and which leads them to truth's eternal abode.

– Upanishads

Truth and non-violence are the two wheels of the chariot of God.
– Mahatma Gandhi

A lie once told is like leprosy, that affects all who come into contact with it.
– Tradition

The damage caused by a false accusation can never be undone, and it causes the speaker to be reborn as a ghost.
– Tradition

He who in his conduct persevere a mind free from deceit will dwell in the hearts of all humans.
– Tradition

Buddhism

Honesty is simple truthfulness in every action of body, speech, and mind. Dishonesty means deceiving others, with our speech or through gestures. Whether motivated by desire, hatred or ignorance, dishonesty creates confusion and entangles us in a web of deceit. Dishonest actions give rise to similar results: we are constantly deceived and cheated. Moral integrity is essential to spiritual progress.

In Tibet, there was a great yogi named Milarepa, the "cotton clad." After his father died when he was a young boy, his aunt and uncle seized his family home and property through treachery. Under the influence of an evil teacher, Milarepa unleashed a hailstorm in revenge, killing a large number of horses and people. Later regretting his action, he began to study the true path under the great teacher Marpa. Years went by, but Marpa only put him to work and never gave him spiritual instruction. Frustrated, Milarepa forged a letter from his teacher and went to seek meditation instruction from another. He meditated with all his might according to these instructions, but was never able to achieve even the slightest realization. After months and months of seeing Milarepa's fruitless practice, the instructor said, "This is very strange! Are you sure you have your teacher's permission?" Confronted like this, Milarepa confessed that he had forged the letter from Marpa. Because his spiritual practice was based on a lie, his efforts were all in vain. Without a foundation of moral integrity, even if he were to practice for 100 years, he would never be able to achieve realization. Realizing his error, he returned to Marpa and confessed all he had done. In time, after Milarepa had purified his negative deeds through years of strenuous effort, Marpa bestowed the highest empowerments and sent Milarepa to the snowy mountain peaks to practice. Dressed only in a thin cotton cloth in the frozen climate of Tibet, Milarepa meditated with sheer determination. Inspired by genuine compassion and unmoved by worldly fame or gain, he practiced persistently until he reached the highest state of enlightenment.

Ethical conduct is the foundation of every success, both mundane and spiritual. To refrain from killing, stealing, and sexual misconduct are the three virtues of body. To refrain from lying, abusive speech, divisive speech, and idle gossip are the four virtues of speech. To refrain from malice, covetousness, and perverted views are the three virtues of mind. A life guided by these ten virtues will be uncomplicated, wholesome, and happy.

Zen Buddhism

It is often said that truth is something that is universally valid. To put it simply, it is something which can be applied anytime, anywhere, and to anyone. For instance, fire is hot no matter what time it is. Fire was hot thousands of years ago, as surely as fire will be hot hundreds of years from now. Of course, fire is hot today. Furthermore, fire is hot in America, and it is hot in Russia as well as in Japan. Fire is hot no matter where.

Christianity

The Two Sons

"What do you think about this? A man with two sons told the older boy, 'Son, go out and work on the farm today.' 'I won't,' he answered, but later he changed his mind and went. Then the father told his youngest, 'You go!' and he said, 'Yes, sir, I will.' But he didn't. Which of the two sons was obeying his father?"

They replied, "The first, of course!"

– Bible, Matthew 21: 28-31

Islam

Verily, truth is goodness, and goodness leads to paradise; and verily lying is wickedness, and wickedness leads to the fire (of hell).

– Selections from Mishkat-ul-masabi [928] p. 208
Ibni Mas'ud, MU

Chinese

"I do not see what use a man can be put to, whose word cannot be trusted. How can a wagon be made to go if it has no yoke-bar or a carriage if it has no collar-bar?"

– Confucius

"In the old days a man kept a hold on his words, fearing the disgrace that would ensue should he himself fail to keep pace with them."

– Confucius

"The Tao buddeth forth all things under heaven; it is the Mother of all."

– Lao Tzu

The Master said, "How can we call even Weisheng Kao upright? When someone asked him for vinegar he went and begged it from the people next door, and then gave it as though it were his own gift."

– The Analects, Book V

The Master said, "in vain have I looked for a single man capable of seeing his own faults and bringing the charge home against himself."

– The Analects, Book V

Were I discovered by men and charged with government, my first fear would be lest I should become proud. The true Path is level and smooth; but men love by paths.

They adorn their courts, but they neglect their fields, and leave their stockhouses empty. They wear elaborate and embroidered robes; they gird themselves with sharp swords; they eat and drink with luxury; they heap up goods; they are thieves and vainglorious. All this is opposite to the Way of Tao.

– Tao Te Ching

The Empty Pot

Long, long ago in China, there was a boy named Ping. More than anything else in the world, Ping loved flowers and had the gift of being able to make anything grow. He could plant any seed and up would grow beautiful blossoms and rich green leaves. Ping's family and friends would marvel at the wonderful things he was able to grow.

Now, the Emperor in those days was also a great lover of flowers and loved to spend time in his garden, which was filled with beautiful shrubs and fine fruit trees. Each day he would tend to all the lovely things growing there.

But unfortunately, the good Emperor was growing old and was becoming more and more worried about finding someone who would rule fairly after he was gone. How should he choose someone, he wondered daily. Finally, he decided that because he loved flowers so much, he would let the flowers do the choosing.

The very next day, the Emperor issued a proclamation throughout the land. All the children in the realm were to come to the palace. Each child would be given special flower seeds to plant. "Whoever returns with the best in a year's time will inherit my throne!" were the Emperor's words.

Everyone was so excited by the possibilities, and the next day all the children of the land gathered in a long line to await their seeds from the Emperor.

Ping, so anxious to have something to grow for the Emperor, traveled the long distance from his home to the palace. He waited patiently in the long line until, at last, he gladly received his seed from the Emperor. Ping was overjoyed. He was certain that he would grow the most exquisite flower with such a seed.

When he arrived home, he chose a sturdy pot and filled it with good soil. Each day he watered it lovingly and made sure it got the sunshine it needed. He could not wait to see it sprout and grow into a beautiful flower!

Days passed, and Ping waited patiently, but nothing happened. He became worried and put the seed in a larger pot with more good soil. He watered it carefully and made certain it received sunlight, and still nothing happened. Finally, he put the seed into an even better pot and made sure it had the richest

soil. He continued to care for it, and watched over it for months, yet no sprout came. Month after month Ping tried and waited until finally the year was up.

The day had arrived for all the children to return to the palace with the flowers they had grown. They flooded toward the palace gates, eager to be chosen as the next emperor. Ping watched as children with azaleas, peonies, and chrysanthemums streamed by. He saw roses and lilies and orchids like he had never seen before. He was so ashamed of his empty pot. He could not believe that for once he had not been able to make a flower grow.

Just then his friend passed by, holding a beautiful white lily. "Ping!" he cried. "What are you doing with that empty pot? Couldn't you grow anything at all? I'm on my way to the palace with this great big flower now. Where's yours?" The boy did not wait for Ping to answer. He sped off to see if he would be chosen by the Emperor.

A tear trickled slowly down Ping's cheek. "I've grown many flowers before," he said to himself. "I don't know why this seed would not grow."

Ping's father heard Ping's sad words. He placed his hand on Ping's shoulder and said, "Son, you did your very best, and that is good enough for the Emperor. If the best you could do is in that empty pot, then that is what you must show him."

Nodding, Ping picked up the empty pot and headed directly for the palace.

When he arrived there, the Emperor was already examining the hundreds of flowers brought by the eager children. He stopped at each one, but said nothing.

Finally, he came to Ping and his empty pot. Ping hung his head, hoping that the Emperor would not be angry with him.

The Emperor spoke to Ping. "Why did you bring me an empty pot?"

Tears trickled once again down Ping's cheeks. With his head bowed he replied, "I planted the seed you gave me. I gave it a nice pot with good soil. I watered it each day, but it did not sprout. I put it in a better pot with rich, dark soil. I cared for it lovingly for a year and still it did not grow. So all I have to show you is an empty pot. It is the best I can do."

A smile swept across the Emperor's face and holding Ping's hand high in the air he exclaimed, "I have found him! I have found the next emperor! It is this boy and this boy alone who is worthy!" Then he spoke sternly to all the other children who had gathered with their flowers. "I do not know where the seeds for all of your beautiful flowers came from, for the seeds I gave you had all been cooked, making it impossible for them to grow." Placing his hand upon Ping's shoulder, the Emperor said proudly, "Ping is the only one who returned to me with the truth in his empty pot. It is for his courage and honesty that I reward him with my kingdom and my throne!"

Hawaii

The Lost Kapa Beater

Kalei had lost her favorite kapa beater. In ancient Hawaii, a kapa beater was a very important implement for the women since women were the ones who were responsible for the hard work of pounding the water-soaked strips of bark from mulberry shrubs, which became clothing for their families.

Kalei looked everywhere for her kapa beater, which looked like a small club with intricate designs carved into it. It had a unique sound, which only she could recognize, and as she walked from one end of the island of Oahu to the other, listening to the women in their villages pounding kapa, she listened for the sound of her kapa beater. She had traveled all day and all night and was tired, so she finally stopped to rest under a tree.

The exhausted woman soon slept, and in her sleep a soft breeze carried a faint sound of the pounding of a kapa beater. She quickly awakened and realized the sound was carried by a gentle breeze, which was coming from the mountains to the valley where she had stopped to rest.

The sound was familiar to Kalei, and she began to walk in the direction from which it came. As she walked, the sound became louder and louder. It was a sound that was so dear to her she began to cry, knowing that she would soon see her beloved kapa beater again. For awhile she had to walk beside a stream which eventually led her to a cave where a woman was pounding her kapa with Kalei's kapa beater. Kalei spoke to the woman, "That sounds like my kapa beater. How did you get it?" The woman reluctantly gave the club back to Kalei, replying, "I found it floating in the stream which flows from the mountain."

The woman followed Kalei back to her home, on the other side of the island far from the mountain cave, to see if Kalei was being honest. When she reached Kalei's village she tied a bundle of large leaves together and tossed it into the stream near Kalei's home, then returned to her mountain cave.

After a few days the woman saw the bundle of leaves floating in the stream near her home and was satisfied that Kalei was indeed the owner of the kapa beater she had found.

PROVERBS AND MAXIMS

We must love them both—those whose opinions we share, and those whose opinions we reject. For both have labored in the search for Truth and both have helped us in the finding of it.
— *St. Thomas Aquinas*

Truth exists;
only falsehood has to be invented.
— *George Braque*

Ignorance is preferable to error, and he is less remote from the truth who believes nothing than he who believes what is wrong.
— *Thomas Jefferson*

If you tell the truth, you have infinite power supporting you; but if not, you have infinite power against you.
— *Charles Gordon*

As scarce as truth is, the supply has always been in excess of the demand.
— *H. W. Shaw*

HEROES AND HEROINES

DIETRICH BONHOEFFER (1906–1945)

Born in Breslau, Germany, he moved with his family to Berlin when he was six. He received his doctorate in Theology from Berlin University when he was only twenty-one. After one year as pastor of a church and one year at Union Theological Seminary in New York City, he returned to Berlin University, where he became a lecturer in Theology. His writing had a major influence on post-World War II Protestant Theology. He could easily be an example of the values of commitment, courage, faith, freedom, or peace, but he is mentioned under honesty because he spoke the truth during a time when it would have been safer to lie. He was one of the first German Protestants to see the evil of Nazism and speak out publicly against Hitler. He called for Christian involvement and was executed by the Nazis for his actions.

CONFUCIUS (551 B.C.E.–478 B.C.E.)

Born as Kung Fu-Tze (Confucius is a translation into Latin) in what is now Shantung, China, he probably wasn't religious in the traditional sense, yet many scholars consider him a holy man. Confucius considered himself a teacher of four basic subjects: literature, human conduct, being one's true self, and honesty in social relationships. The heart of his teachings was what he called "shu": "Do not do unto others what you would not have others do unto you." Confucius strongly believed that a person's first duty was to be virtuous; this would create a strong community of harmony and peace. Though more philosopher than theologian, his ideas about morality became the state religion of China—Confucianism.

COCHISE (1815–1874)

Born in the mountains of southern Arizona, this Native American followed in a long line of Chiricahua Apache chiefs. He was both feared and respected as a leader, and was chief of the Chiricahuas during the time white settlers were trying to take their homeland. Cochise was raised in the ancient tradition of leadership that encompassed both war and peace. Until the white settlers broke their trust, Cochise maintained a relationship of peace and was known for his honor and for keeping his word. Before he died he affirmed the importance of truth and honesty even to those who were untrustworthy. He urged his sons to maintain the peace and always be honest; this would be an example of the honorable way to live.

BARBARA JORDAN (1936–1996)

Born in Houston, Texas into a very poor home, she and her sister were reared in a strict family. Her father was a Baptist minister and her mother was trained as an orator in the church. As a child, she showed a talent for public speaking and became the star of her high school debating team. While she had interests in pharmacy, she changed her mind upon hearing a black woman attorney speak at her school's career day. She graduated with honors in political science and history from Texas Southern University and entered Boston Law School in 1956. She was the first black woman to be elected to the Texas Senate and credited her success to a personal interest in the people and a dedication to speaking the truth. She was elected to the U.S. House of Representatives in 1972. She is remembered as a champion for the poor, a hero to the oppressed, and a model for anyone who aspires to be an honest politician.

MARTIN LUTHER (1483–1546)

Born in Eisleben, Germany, he was the son of peasant parents who worked hard to give him a good education. Two career fields were open to educated people: the law and the church. Hans Luther, Martin's father, was anti-church, and pushed Martin toward law; by 1505 he was well on his way. However, Martin experienced a religious crisis and, out of fear, decided to become a priest. He received his doctorate in theology in 1512 and was destined to teach theology all his life. His basic honesty did not allow him to turn his back on the dishonesty of the Church and his disagreements with Church theology. In 1521, he was brought to trial and had to choose between his personal views and the will of the Church. His decision forced his removal from the priesthood and he became instrumental in the Protestant Reformation. He is perhaps the greatest figure of the Reformation and is still a symbol of honesty and moral courage.

PUT HONESTY INTO ACTION

- Admit a mistake you've made and apologize to anyone it might have affected.

- Do all your schoolwork honestly and as best as you can.

- Be truthful with your friends and thank them for being truthful with you.

- When you ask someone to be honest with you, don't get angry with them if their honesty isn't what you wanted to hear.

- Speak with kindness against cheating and stealing when someone talks about it.

- Be completely honest about a mistake you've made, avoiding partial truths and exaggeration.

- Do the right thing, even when no one is looking.

- Call a foul on yourself; ask your coach to support you.

COMMUNITY SERVICE IDEAS

- Write a letter of thanks to a politician or community leader who has taken a stand on a controversial issue.

- Organize a field trip to a local park for people with disabilities.

- Organize a drive for clothing, stuffed animals, and books for Child and Family Service.

- Volunteer with the Judiciary Volunteers in Public Service to the Courts as an information guide or office work.

- Volunteer at a hospital to read stories such as *The Emperor's New Clothes* or play board games with the elderly.

- Make tray favors with cheerful slogans related to honesty for patients in a hospital.

BOOKS ON HONESTY

Anansi and the Moss Covered Rock. Janet Stevens. New York: Holiday House, 1988.

Strega Nona. Tomie De Paola. Englewood Cliffs: Prentice Hall, 1975.

True Francine. Marc T. Brown. Boston: Little, Brown, 1972.

True Story of the 3 Little Pigs! Lane Smith. New York: Viking Kestrel, 1989.

The Book of Virtues. William J. Bennett, ed. New York: Simon and Schuster, 1993.

 "The Emperor's New Clothes" – p. 630

 "The Frog Prince" – p. 623

 "The Good Bishop" – p. 644

 "Honest Abe" – p. 620

 "The Indian Cinderella" – p. 612

 "The Piece of String" – p. 648

 "Pinocchio" – p. 609

 "The Story of Regalus" – p. 617

Cooperation

SUPPORTIVE VALUES

Family • Unity

DEFINITIONS

Common effort of a group for their mutual benefit.

"There is no 'I' in team." "United we stand, divided we fall." "No man is an island." If all of these statements speak to the importance of cooperation, to the idea that we live interdependently, it is then necessary that we do so as effectively as possible. **Cooperation** is as much a cornerstone of this country as is independence, and both values, as paradoxical as it seems, are highly honored in our society.

Family is commonly defined as a group of people who share common ancestors. In a broader sense, family can also include all people everywhere, by virtue of our common link as human beings. Montaigne said, "Every man beareth the stamp of the whole human condition." The nuclear family, extended family, and the family of humanity are the focus of the partner value, family.

Unity connotes oneness. Unity is what is required for cooperation and for a well-functioning family.

PURPOSE

As our world becomes smaller, as a result of mass communication and our networking technology, we are becoming more aware of how necessary it is, for our own survival, to work with other people cooperatively. Competition has long been the driving force of our democratic society; yet if we look at the history of this country we see that it was cooperative effort which created and continues to sustain America.

"The whole is greater than the sum of its parts," speaks to the importance and the strength derived from unity. We also know that in creating a team, or a unified effort of any kind, it is wiser to stay together than stand as individuals.

The importance of understanding that we are interconnected with our environment as well as interdependent with humanity is an understanding without which we cannot survive as a species. The demand for cooperation in the world is obvious and has already affected the way most educators conduct classes. The rewards of cooperation are numerous; as we move our students out of their sometimes self-centered molds and have them work with others, we reinforce many of the preceding values which are inherent in the cooperative process. The Sioux state these ideas simply: "With all beings and all things we shall be as relatives."

Cooperation

Day One: In a total class setting, discuss the meaning of cooperation based on the definitions on page 33 as compared to your own definition of cooperation.	**Day Two:** What does "many hands make for light work" mean to you? Draw a picture.	**Day Three:** With your classmates, create a list of things that people do which take cooperation. (Here's a few to get you started: present a play, play soccer, build a bridge.)	**Day Four:** Conduct a three-legged race. The pair that cooperates the best nearly always wins! Name some other sporting events where this is also true.	**Day Five:** Create a "Pear of the Week" award to present to two students whose cooperation serves as an example for others. Make a pear tree to hang the "Pear" award on each week. Add pears to the tree all month.
Day Six: Read one of the stories about cooperation on pages 37–44. Make a list of discussion questions to use with the story to demonstrate the value of cooperation.	**Day Seven:** Use what you have learned so far about cooperation to answer the discussion questions on page 36. Plan a panel discussion suitable for radio or t.v. based on the questions.	**Day Eight:** Write a short story about a village where no one cooperates with each other. What limits are placed on the lives of these people?	**Day Nine:** Research an animal species which depends on cooperation for survival. Some examples are: Canadian Geese (flying), Humpback whales (bubble feeding tube), Wolves (hunt in packs), and Fish (swim in schools for protection). Share with your classmates the information you learn.	**Day Ten:** Embrace the spirit of cooperation by completing a homework assignment with a partner. How much time would you estimate was saved through your cooperative efforts? How did you use this extra time?
Day Eleven: Determine to demonstrate the power of cooperation today! Think of one way you can cooperate with another person either at school or at home and then do it!	**Day Twelve:** Draw a picture or write about your experience yesterday with cooperation. Display and marvel at all the different ways your classmates cooperated with others!	**Day Thirteen:** Read about the heroes and heroines of cooperation on pages 46–47. What would our world be like today if these people had not embraced the value of cooperation? Write a short original story describing how they impacted the world beyond their own lifetime.	**Day Fourteen:** Choose, color, and cut out a bookmark on page 45. Choose a book to keep it in to remind you of the value of cooperation.	**Day Fifteen:** Think of a time when you were faced with a challenge. Did others cooperate with you to help you overcome this challenge? If not, think of how you may enlist the cooperative efforts of others the next time you need help to overcome a challenge.
Day Sixteen: This week cooperate with your classmates to organize a community service project. Choose one from page 48, divide the responsibilities, and then make plans to carry it out!	**Day Seventeen:** Carry out your service project.	**Day Eighteen:** Evaluate the outcome of your service project to determine how well members of the class cooperated with each other to make it as successful as possible. What would you do differently next time?	**Day Nineteen:** Cooperate with your classmates to create a harvest festival celebration for your classroom. Invite other classes to enjoy the seasonal flavor!	**Day Twenty:** Review the lessons you have learned this month about cooperation and reflect on how you can begin now to embrace it as a lifelong value!

COOPERATION IN OTHER LANGUAGES

Chinese	*xie*	united in; agreement; mutual help; to aid; to help
	li	power; strength
French	*la cooperation*	collaboration with others; to act jointly with someone
German	*zusammenarbeit*	to work together
Hawaiian	*laulima*	cooperation, joint action (lau means "very many, numerous" and lima means "arm, hand")
Japanese	*kyooryoku*	to put everyone's ability and energy into one kyoo— put power and energy into one ryoku—power, energy, ability
Korean	*hyup dong*	together and same
Latin	*adiumentum*	from Latin "cum" (together with) + "opus" (work) (working together)
Spanish	*cooperación*	cooperation
Tagalog	*pakikiisa*	united effort or labor; working together to accomplish what can't be done alone

*C*ooperation———————————LEARNING ABOUT

DISCUSSION QUESTIONS

- As competition in sports provides motivation to do the best we can, can cooperation provide similar motivation for the good of the community?

- How big is your family? Is it possible to create a human family of all the people of the world?

- How is the future of our planet connected with the way in which we live in harmony with all creation?

- What do you like best about the teamwork aspect of sports?

- Do you think American society has developed a proper balance between cooperation and competition?

- How far can we extend the concept of family? The community? America? The world? Why does it become more difficult?

STORIES AND THOUGHTS FROM SPIRITUAL TRADITIONS

Hinduism

The joys of liberation are for then, the joys of a loving family are for now.

– Tradition

Never may brother hate brother or sister hurt sister. United in heart and in purpose, commune sweetly together.

– Atharva Veda

Buddhism

Cooperation comes through realizing the interdependence of all living beings.

Once there were four friends: an elephant, a rabbit, a monkey, and a bird. Each of them looked enviously at the ripe mango fruits high on the treetops. They each in turn tried with all their might to get to the fruits hanging on the branches, but the fruits were too high to reach. Finally, they hit upon a plan. With a little cooperation, they could all eat their fill. First, the elephant stood sturdily at the base of the tree. Then the monkey helped the rabbit climb up on the elephant's back. Then the monkey leaped up and stood on the rabbit's back. Finally, the bird perched on the monkey's back. Collaborating like this, the four friends were able to pluck one ripe mango after the other and pass them along until everyone got to eat as many mangoes as they liked!

Zen Buddhism

For instance, water is known as H_2O. It consists of the mixture of hydrogen and oxygen at the ratio of two to one. However, it is impossible for us to drink only the oxygen or the hydrogen part of water. They say that the bird named hamsa-raja is capable of separating water from milk and drinking only concentrated milk. We human beings, however, cannot perform such a feat. The analysis of human beings in terms of individuals, classes, or races certainly serves to deepen our view of human beings. However, the one-sided emphasis on any particular one of the above groups with the exclusion of others is undesirable. There is no other way to reward such men of inflexible thought than by commanding them to drink the hydrogen component of water alone, if indeed they can.

Cooperation —————————— UNDERSTANDING

Christianity

"How good and pleasant it is when brothers and sisters live together in unity."
– Psalm 133:1

"If one member suffers, all suffer together; if one member is honored, all rejoice together."
– Bible, I Corinthians 12:26

"Working together we encourage you to accept the Grace of God."
– Bible, II Corinthians 6:1

Joshua and Jericho

The Gates of Jericho were kept tightly shut because the people were afraid of the Israelis; no one was allowed to go in or out.

But the Lord said to Joshua, "Jericho and its king and all its mighty warriors are already defeated, for I have given them to you! Your entire army is to walk around the city once a day for six days, followed by seven priests walking ahead of the Ark, each carrying a trumpet made from a ram's horn. On the seventh day you are to walk around the city seven times, with the priests blowing their trumpets. Then, when they give one long, loud blast, all the people are to give a mighty shout and the walls of the city will fall down; then move in upon the city from every direction."

So Joshua summoned the priests and gave them their instructions: the armed men would lead the procession followed by seven priests blowing continually on their trumpets. Behind them would come the priests carrying the Ark, followed by a rear guard.

"Let there be complete silence except for the trumpets," Joshua commanded. "Not a single word from any of you until I tell you to shout; then shout!"

The Ark was carried around the city once that day, after which everyone returned to the camp again and spent the night there.

At dawn the next morning they went around again, and returned again to the camp. They followed this pattern for six days. At dawn of the seventh day they started out again, but this time they went around the city not once, but seven times. The seventh time, as the priests blew a long, loud trumpet blast, Joshua yelled to the people, "Shout! The Lord has given us the city!"

So when the people heard the trumpet blast, they shouted as loud as they could. And suddenly the walls of Jericho crumbled and fell before them, and the people of Israel poured into the city from every side and captured it!
– Bible, Joshua 6:1-16, 20-21

Islam

The master next told a story about Shaykh Najib ad-din Mutawakkil—may God have mercy upon him. "Many times he wanted to set to writing a compilation of Sufi anecdotes, but his income was so tight that he could not manage to purchase the instrument for writing and also to pay wages for a scribe; if a scribe did become available, he could not afford to pay him, or if he somehow found the means to pay him, he could not obtain additional funds to buy paper and the other provisions necessary for writing. Then one day a scribe named Hamid came to him. Shaykh Najib ad-din told him: 'For a long time now I have wanted to commit to writing a compilation of Sufi anecdotes, but I have not found the means to accomplish that objective.' 'What are your present resources?' asked Hamid. 'I have one diram [a silver coin equivalent to about 4 cents],' replied Shaykh Najib ad-din. Hamid took that one diram and bought paper with it. Now everyone knows how little paper one diram can buy, and Hamid had not finished writing on that paper before Shaykh Najib ad-din received another charitable donation, with which he purchased more paper and the other necessities for writing. Money for the scribe's salary also came to hand. More and more charitable donations continued to arrive, and as a result the book was quickly and satisfactorily completed. The point is: Even a work begun with difficulty will be completed, as long as one persists; and without cooperation, the book could not have been completed."

– Nizam Ad-Din Awliya: Morals of the Heart p. 110
I. Assembly 26
Saturday, the 23rd of Ramadan, A.H. 708 (15 March 1309)

Our treatment of our fellow human beings must always be in accord with our common humanity. The surah of this verse was delivered nine years after the migration to Madinah, at a time when the Muslim community was growing rapidly, drawing on the peoples of many different tribes. It was known as the Year of Deputations, for by now representatives of diverse tribal and political interests were visiting the Prophet in official recognition of Islam. It was at this time of Islam's increasing power that Allah enjoined us to remember that we are brothers and sisters, descended from the first man and woman He created. The importance of this injunction has continued to grow as Islam's role in the world has grown.

– The Essential Teachings of Islam p. 207
320: The Inner Apartments (Hujurat) 49:13

Character Education Year 2 Grades 6–12 **39**

Let there arise among you an ummat advocating all that is good, enjoining what is right and forbidding what is wrong. They are the ones to attain peace and prosperity.

The word ummat is not easily translated, as it embraces the concepts of brotherhood, community, nation, religion, and way of life. The ummat is central to Islam as a religion that includes love of humanity out of love of Allah. Islam is not a religion of the hermit or the ascetic, cut off from his fellow men and daily life. Indeed, worship of Allah and work in His Cause is synonymous [sic] with community life.

> *– The Essential Teachings of Islam p. 206*
> *318: The Family of Imran (Al-i-imran) 3:104*

O Mankind, We created you from a single male and female and made you into nations and tribes so that you may come to know each other. Truly the most honoured of you in the sight of Allah is the most righteous of you. And Allah has full knowledge and is well aware.

Chinese

"He who sets to work upon a different strand destroys the whole fabric."

> *– Confucius*

"Moral force never dwells in solitude; it will always bring neighbors."

> *– Confucius*

"Simplicity in the doing of the will of every person would put an end to vain ambitions and desires."

> *– Lao Tzu*

"He who understands others understands Two; but he who understands himself understands One."

> *– Lao Tzu*

The Master said, The case is like that of someone raising a mound. If he stops working, the fact that it perhaps needed only one more basketful makes no difference; I stay where I am. Whereas even if he has not got beyond leveling the ground, but is still at work, the fact that he has only tilted one basketful of earth makes no difference. I go to help him.

> *– The Analects, Book IX*

India

The Little Squirrel Becomes a Savior

On the branches of an old banyan tree in the forest lived a squirrel couple. A bonny child was born to them. It was as handsome as it was frolicsome.

"He ought to grow up into a remarkable creature—remain a squirrel like us forever," his mother told his father.

"Yes, he has every sign of becoming great—like one of those deer here," agreed the little one's father. He did not wish his son to become anything else because they had not known any other animal. And because the deer had hair and stripes like those of the squirrels, the squirrel couple thought that they were just bigger squirrels though known as deer!

"But how can he grow up to become a deer?" asked the mother squirrel.

"Well, how do other kids grow into deer? There must be some method," observed the father squirrel. He was always logical like this and the mother squirrel could not contest his wisdom. "Better we ask them," she said.

At night a herd of deer slept around the banyan tree, amidst bushes. The place was surrounded by rocks or tall anthills, with very few openings. So, they considered the cozy place quite safe.

It was a moonlit night. The deer gathered there as usual. The squirrel couple addressed them from a branch of the banyan tree and told them all about their ambition regarding their son, drawing their attention to the little one.

The first to speak was a hefty deer. "I too was a little squirrel when I was born. But through sheer willpower I grew to what I am."

"And look at me," rejoined a heftier deer, "I grew up to this stature through regular exercise, discipline and wrestling with some stout boars."

"And if all the tigers of the forest are scared of me today, it is because I have gathered more muscle-power than them," said a third deer who was no less hefty.

The squirrels, of course, did not know what was meant by 'tigers.' Nevertheless, they were impressed.

"That is fine, but how can our little baby become like you? What should he do, to begin with?" asked the mother squirrel.

"To begin with? Hm!" said the hefty deer.

"Well, to begin with, um, um . . . " the heftier deer stopped there.

"It is late enough tonight. We will pass on the secret to you another time," said the no-less-hefty deer, and he added in a commanding voice, "Now, all to sleep!"

And all fell asleep—but not the little squirrel. He kept on gazing at the deer. He wondered how they could become so big. Yes, they too had stripes and they too had hair like his parents, though their hair differed slightly in color.

His parents were asleep. He hopped down to a bush and then leaped on to a rock to have a closer look at the deer. But what did he see? Two human beings were stealthily doing something. He knew the human beings to be very clever animals who lived outside the forest. He observed that these two human beings had closed all the openings with their nets. They were now putting a finishing touch to closing the last opening.

Why were they doing this? Surely not to catch the squirrels! They must be planning to catch the deer. They worked so cautiously and quietly that no deer was aware of the terrible fate awaiting them.

As one of the humans was tying the last knot, the little squirrel jumped onto his nose. The man gave out an involuntary shriek. The net fell from his hand. The deer woke up. They found all the openings shut, but got away through the solitary opening which had not been shut. The little squirrel's parents too had awakened. They became anxious when they found that their son was missing. But soon the little one was back with them, and told them what he had done.

An old owl, who lived in the hollow of a neem tree opposite, told the deerfolk when they were back, "You loudmouths! What happened to your muscle-flexing and frightening the tigers? Today all of you would have been captured by the human beings. You would have been killed for flesh or imprisoned in a zoo. The little squirrel saved you. Bow to him and confess your lies to him. Nature has made him a squirrel as Nature has made you deer and made me an owl. Our ideal should be to be good and brave, not to become someone else. Just as a squirrel can be a noble squirrel, a deer can be an ignoble deer or vice versa."

The deer stood ashamed. They apologized to the squirrels.

Judaism

The Strength of Community

The Baal Shem was very troubled because the clouds had hidden the moon and it was time for him to say the Blessing of the Moon after the Day of Atonement. He struggled with all of his power to bring the moon from behind the cover of clouds. His followers knew nothing of their master's struggle and joyfully danced just as they did every year at this time. They came into his room where they ignored his gloomy state and pleaded with him to join in the dance. All of a sudden someone called from outside. The moon had finally emerged from beneath her blanket and showered the night in her luminous glow. The strength of the community was more powerful than the master's solitary efforts.

Russian

The Turnip

Once upon a time, there lived a very old man called Dedoushka. He had lots of land and he loved to farm it. One day as he was walking through his fields he came upon a single turnip seed. "Ah!" he declared joyfully, "What a wonderful little gift! I shall find the perfect place to plant it so that it can grow very large indeed."

He hobbled up to the top of a little hill where he knew it would get just the right amount of sun and rain. He dug a little hole in the earth, placed the turnip seed in it and covered it ever so carefully again with soil. Each day Dedoushka would gaze out upon the little hill, knowing that the sun was shining on the turnip, and the rain was watering the turnip, and soon it would be very large indeed.

Finally, after many days of waiting, Dedoushka set out for the top of the hill. There he found that his turnip had grown very, very large indeed!

"Ah!" he cried, "What an enormous turnip!" He reached down to pull the gigantic turnip from the earth. He pulled and he pulled, and finally he sighed, "Oh, this turnip is too large. I must call my dear wife Baboushka. Baboushka! Baboushka!" Dedoushka called loudly.

"Yes, my darling," answered Baboushka.

"You must come and help me with this turnip. It is very, very large!" cried Dedoushka.

"Of course, my darling," replied Baboushka and she started up the hill. When she got to the top, she exclaimed, "Ah! What an enormous turnip!"

So Baboushka pulled Dedoushka, and Dedoushka pulled the turnip. They pulled and they pulled, but the turnip would not budge. "Oh, this turnip is too large. We must call our granddaughter, Mashenka. Mashenka! Mashenka!" Baboushka called loudly.

"Yes, dear grandmother," answered Mashenka.

"You must come and help us with this turnip. It is very, very large!" cried Baboushka.

"Of course, dear grandmother," replied Mashenka, and she started up the hill. When she got to the top, she exclaimed, "What an enormous turnip!"

So Mashenka pulled Baboushka, and Baboushka pulled Dedoushka, and Dedoushka pulled the turnip. They pulled and they pulled, but the turnip would not budge. "Oh, this turnip is too large. We must call our little dog Geoutchka. Geoutchka! Geoutchka!" Mashenka called loudly.

"Yes, mistress," answered the little dog, Geoutchka.

"You must come and help us with this turnip. It is very, very large!" cried Mashenka.

"Of course, mistress," replied Geoutchka. He ran up to the top of the hill and when he saw the turnip he exclaimed, "Oh mistress, what an enormous turnip!"

So Geoutchka pulled Mashenka, Mashenka pulled Baboushka, Baboushka pulled Dedoushka, and Dedoushka pulled the turnip. They pulled and they pulled, but the turnip would not budge.

"Oh, this turnip is too large. We must call our little friend, Keska, the cat. Keska, oh Keska!" cried Geoutchka loudly.

"Oh, what is it now?" yawned Keska, the cat. "Why must you wake me from my nap?"

"You must come and help us with this turnip. It is very, very large!" cried Geoutchka from the top of the hill.

"Oh, I suppose I can help, now that I am awake," said Keska, as she wound her way leisurely to the top of the hill. When she saw the turnip she exclaimed, "What an enormous turnip! And what delicious soup it will make!"

So Keska pulled Geoutchka, Geoutchka pulled Mashenka, Mashenka pulled Baboushka, Baboushka pulled Dedoushka, and Dedoushka pulled the turnip. They pulled and they pulled, but the turnip would not budge.

"Oh, how ridiculous! This turnip will never come out," cried Keska in dismay.

"Yes, it will," insisted Dedoushka. "We must call the little field mouse to help."

"The little field mouse?" the others chorused in surprise. "Why should we bother calling the little field mouse for help?"

"Because we need just a little more help, of course," replied Dedoushka. "Little field mouse! Oh, little field mouse!" Dedoushka called loudly.

"Yes. What can I do for you?" squeaked the little field mouse.

"You must come and help us with this turnip. It is very, very large. If we all try together I am sure we can pull it out and then we will have the most delicious turnip soup for supper," declared Dedoushka.

"Of course, I will help," said the little field mouse as he scampered to the top of the hill. "Oh my, what an enormous turnip!" said the little field mouse as he reached the others. "Let's pull!"

So the little field mouse pulled Keska, Keska pulled Geoutchka, Geoutchka pulled Mashenka, Mashenka pulled Baboushka, Baboushka pulled Dedoushka, and Dedoushka pulled the turnip. They pulled and they pulled—and out popped the turnip!

"You see," cried Dedoushka, "I told you we could do it together! Now together we will eat the most delicious turnip soup!"

PROVERBS AND MAXIMS

We may have all come on different ships, but we're in the same boat now.

— *Martin Luther King, Jr.*

Behold how good and
how pleasant it is for brethren
to dwell together in unity.

— *Psalms 133:1*

We cannot live only for ourselves. A thousand fibers connect us with our fellow men; and among those fibers, as sympathetic threads, our actions run as causes, and they come back to us as effects. — *Herman Melville*

There is no more sure tie between friends than when they are united in their objects and wishes.

— *Cicero*

There are many objects of great value to man which cannot be attained by unconnected individuals, but must be attained, if at all, by association.

— *Daniel Webster*

HEROES AND HEROINES

DAG HAMMARSKJÖLD (1905–1961)

Born in Jönköping, Sweden into one of Sweden's oldest families, Dag grew up in Uppsala, Sweden, where his father was a provincial governor. He earned a law degree from Uppsala University and a doctorate in political science from the University of Stockholm. He became the vice-chairman of Sweden's delegation to the United Nations in 1952, and a year later was elected Secretary General of the United Nations, a position he held until his death in a plane crash in Zambia while on a peacekeeping mission. He practiced "quiet diplomacy" to reduce conflict. A publication of his journal, *Markings*, revealed him as an intensely religious person who was concerned with the contrast between the ideal of world peace and the reality of human frailty. He was awarded the Nobel Peace Prize after his death.

JOHN ROBERT WOODEN (1910–)

Born in Martinsville, Indiana, John Wooden seems to have been destined for a life of basketball. He attended high school there, winning all-prep honors three years in a row and leading his team to the Indiana State title in 1927 and as runner-up in 1926 and 1928. He had a similar career at Purdue University, where he led the Boilermakers to two Big Ten Conference titles and the 1932 NCAA Championship. He began his coaching at Dayton High School in Kentucky, but returned to Indiana, where he coached at South Bend Central High School. After World War II, he went to Indiana Teachers College (now Indiana State University) where he served for two seasons as Athletic Director and basketball and baseball coach. In 1948, he went to the University of California at Los Angeles (UCLA), where he compiled a record that is unsurpassed by any coach in the history of sports. In 40 years of coaching he had an 885–203 win-loss record that is unequaled. His coaching philosophy was built upon a "pyramid of success" that had values like cooperation and friendship at the base, self-control, team spirit and confidence in the center, and honesty, sincerity, patience and faith as supportive values along the side. His honors recognize him not only as a great figure in sports but also as a great humanitarian (1995—Lexington Theological Seminary Service to Mankind Award; 1985—Bellarmine Medal of Excellence; 1995—AYA Humanitarian Award).

MARGARET MEAD (1901–1978)

Born in Philadelphia, Pennsylvania, Margaret grew up in a liberal and highly intellectual home. Her father was a college professor of finance and commerce and her mother was a sociologist and an early advocate of women's rights. Margaret became one of the world's foremost anthropologists and developed research methods that helped turn social anthropology into a major science. She worked with the American Museum of Natural History from 1926 until her death, and taught at Fordham and Columbia. She made expeditions to Samoa, New Guinea, Bali and other parts of the South Pacific, which led to many books and articles that introduced the concept of culture into education, medicine, and character development. She was active in environmental concerns, women's rights, and racial harmony.

RABINDRANATH TAGORE (1861–1941)

Born in Calcutta, India, the youngest of 14 children, he was the son of the "Great Sage," Maharishi Debendranath Tagore. He was educated at home and started writing at an early age. Part of his home schooling was the influence of his father, who worked to purify Hinduism, stressing ethics and service as leading to a direct experience with God. Rabindranath Tagore was known as a gifted and creative artist of abundant gifts; he wrote poetry, short stories, novels, essays, and plays, painted in an unorthodox style, and is considered one of India's best songwriters. His first collection of poems and stories, published in 1890, included his first social and political poems. The influence of his writing and lecturing earned him a reputation in India as an educational, social, and religious reformer on a par with Ghandi. He had a deep concern for social justice and an appreciation for different cultures. He embraced Western Civilization, giving India ways to assimilate the West without becoming a mockery of it. His writing emphasized cooperation between nations, businesses, and religions. He was a myriad-minded man that saw the expressions of beauty within different cultures as a means for stimulating thought, conversation, and action. He dedicated his work to the concept of harmony between people and nations.

WRIGHT BROTHERS (ORVILLE 1871–1948, WILBUR 1867–1912)

Wilbur was born near Millville, Indiana, and Orville was born in Dayton, Ohio. They were the sons of a United Brethren Church Bishop and very early demonstrated abilities in designing and building machines. They opened a bicycle shop and soon became interested in aviation. They started experimenting with gliders, building their first one in 1899. Their first airplane was powered by a twelve-horsepower gasoline engine and was first successfully flown on December 17, 1903 at Kittyhawk, North Carolina. But that was only the beginning, and it took years of patient experimenting before their airplane was perfected. Their third design, built in 1905, could turn in circles and could stay in the air one half-hour. In 1909, they founded an aircraft company and began producing two planes each month, gaining the respect of the entire world. Though Wilbur died of typhoid fever at age 45, Orville enjoyed many years of research. The Wright Brothers gave the world a perfect example of how much people can accomplish when they cooperate and work together.

RALPH BUNCHE (1904–1971)

Born in Detroit, Michigan, the grandson of a slave and the son of a barber, he moved to Los Angeles when he was thirteen, after both of his parents died. He worked his way through the University of California at Los Angeles as a janitor and carpet-layer. He earned a masters and doctorate at Harvard University and taught political science at Howard University from 1928–1942. Because of his knowledge of colonialism and government, he moved to the State Department and then to the United Nations, where he became a trouble-shooter in Palestine, working on the Jewish and Arab disagreements. His efforts led to an armistice in the first Arab-Israeli War, and he became the first African-American to receive the Nobel Peace Prize.

Character Education Year 2 Grades 6–12

PUT COOPERATION INTO ACTION

- Help a younger brother or sister realize the importance of family cooperation.

- Become involved in a community service project.

- Do something to preserve the environment.

- Practice good sportsmanship.

- Compliment someone on being a good sport. Congratulate the winners when you lose and compliment the losers when you win.

- Be unselfish and supportive as a member of a team.

- Organize a community service project.

- Disagree respectfully with someone's opinion and accept their right to believe what they want.

COMMUNITY SERVICE IDEAS

- Collect clothes for Big Brothers and Big Sisters.

- Adopt a beach or park and keep it clean.

- Organize a car wash and give the money to the Red Cross.

- Volunteer for the March of Dimes Halloween project and help create a Haunted House.

- Take training at the Red Cross to help with disaster preparedness.

- Help the American Heart Association with their "Jump Rope for Heart" program.

BOOKS ON COOPERATION

Anansi the Spider. Gerald McDermott. New York: Holt, 1972.

Sam Johnson and the Blue Ribbon Quilt. Lisa C. Ernst. New York: Lothrop, Lee & Shepard Books, 1983.

Stone Soup. Marcia Brown. New York: Atheneum, 1947.

Wilfred Gordon McDonald Partridge. Mem Fox. Brooklyn: Kane/Miller Book Publishers, 1989.

Zinnia and Dot. Lisa C. Ernst. New York: Viking, 1992.

The Book of Virtues. William J. Bennett, ed. New York: Simon and Schuster, 1993.

"Castor and Pollux" – p. 699

"The Devoted Friend" – p. 674

"Knute Rockne" – p. 732

"The Story of Cincinnatus" – p. 671

"Thunder Falls" – p. 686

Chicken Soup for the Teenage Soul. Jack Canfield, et al. Deerfield Beach: Health Communications, Inc., 1997.

"The Gravediggers of Parkview Junior High" – p. 298

"Helen Keller and Anne Sullivan" – p. 294

"Passing the Dream" – p. 273

Humility

SUPPORTIVE VALUES

Gratitude • Appreciation

DEFINITIONS

Having no arrogance, being modest.

Humility, the quality of being humble, without arrogance or pretense, is our focus this month. Modesty is a synonym often used to explain the word humility.

Being pleased, when comfort is given or discomfort alleviated, is certainly a good reason for **gratitude**. It is not the only reason, however. Counting our blessings helps us maintain a positive perspective in life, but being grateful for the opportunities which disguise themselves as problems or tragedies elevates gratitude to another level.

Appreciation is a sense of feeling admiration, approval, or gratitude. Expressing our thanks and being sensitive and aware of ourselves and others is appreciation at its best.

PURPOSE

Humility is a difficult value to define, but you know it when you see it. With the media highlighting arrogant professional athletes and rock stars, it becomes a challenge to support the value of humility. In helping our students realize the talents they are born with, we can encourage them to develop those talents with humility and gratitude and the knowledge that their talents are gifts. In this same way, we can encourage them to be mindful of the many privileges and opportunities they have which they can then learn to humbly appreciate. A little humility would deter the "Life-owes-me-a-living" attitude which is so prevalent in our society.

Too often we take for granted the abundance we have. We are so caught up in our own lives that we don't take the time to truly appreciate our blessings and those events in our lives which present themselves as problems, but are really challenges and opportunities for our own personal growth. Giving with the knowledge of our abundance becomes an expression of humility, gratitude, and appreciation.

Day One:
Write the definition of humility as it first occurs to you. Then write three synonyms and three antonyms.

Day Two:
In a group setting, discuss the meaning of humility using the definitions on page 51 and compare individual student definitions from yesterday with those given.

Day Three:
Work in groups of three to use key words from the definitions and the word lists (antonyms and synonyms) to create a word find or crossword puzzle.

Day Four:
Exchange puzzles from yesterday and work on them. When complete, display for the class to see. Or copy all the puzzles and make a book for each student to solve individually.

Day Five:
To further your understanding of humility answer the discussion questions on page 54.

Day Six:
Thinking of antonyms to humility, tell why humility is a treasured value while arrogance is not.

Day Seven:
Choose two bookmarks from page 65 to decorate and cut out. Save them for later.

Day Eight:
Think of a person whose humble spirit you appreciate. Write to that person and tell him or her of your appreciation. Include with the letter one of the bookmarks you decorated.

Day Nine:
One way we show humility is through expressing gratitude to another person. Think of a person for whom you have deep gratitude. Write a short note telling this person why you feel gratitude for him or her. Include the other bookmark which you created earlier.

Day Ten:
People show their gratitude in different ways. How many can you name (for example, singing, praying, writing thank yous, sending gifts, etc.)?

Day Eleven:
Read and discuss the stories about humility on pages 55–64.

Day Twelve:
Offer to read one of the stories you read yesterday to a younger class or a family member.

Day Thirteen:
What are the benefits of humility? Explore the lives of the heroes and heroines of humility on pages 66–67. How did humility affect their lives for the better?

Day Fourteen:
Does being humble mean you can never exhibit pride in your accomplishments? How can you balance the important values of humility and self-respect?

Day Fifteen:
Do you know the Thanksgiving story? It was a celebration of appreciation and gratitude! Plan to re-create the original thanksgiving feast.

Day Sixteen:
Native Americans showed great humility when they shared their knowledge of agriculture with the Puritans and the Puritans exhibited gratitude by sharing their feast. Do you know this story? Draw a picture of the indians helping the new settlers.

Day Seventeen:
Many religious groups profess that believers are to be humble before god. What does that mean to you? Write your thoughts in a journal entry.

Day Eighteen:
Plan a service project for the specific purpose of sharing the talents and abilities of class members to spread Thanksgiving joy in a grateful and humble manner.

Day Nineteen:
Based on what you have learned this month about humility, as a class, create your own definition of humility. Create a poster or banner to display for the rest of the year.

Day Twenty:
Reflect on what you have learned about humility, and endeavor to embrace it as a lifelong value.

HUMILITY IN OTHER LANGUAGES

Chinese	*qian*	retiring, humble, modest;
	xu	hollow, empty, vacant; pure, unprejudiced, humble
French	*l'humilité*	state of mind or attitude of a person who looks honestly at him/herself without denying his/her faults and tends to downplay his/her own merits or worthiness
German	*bescheidenheit*	modesty, diffidence, discretion, demureness, moderation
Hawaiian	*ha'aha'a*	low, lowly, humble
Japanese	*kenkyo*	to respect with pure mind and not say mean words ken—to be humble kyo—empty, do not have malicious intention
Korean	*kyum son*	self-effacement, modesty
Latin	*humilitas*	from Latin "humilis" (lowly); from "humus" (ground) (having eyes to the ground)
Spanish	*humildad*	humility, humbleness
Tagalog	*kababaang-loob*	a lack of pride; meekness

DISCUSSION QUESTIONS

- What are people saying about themselves when they try to be the center of attention?

- Can a person be proud and humble at the same time?

- Make a list of things for which you are thankful. How many relate to your physical comfort? How many are about relationships? How many are spiritual? Is there a good balance?

- How do you express your appreciation of these blessings?

- How much do you share with others?

- How can you turn challenges and difficulties into positive opportunities?

- Why is it hard to get along with someone who is always boasting of their accomplishments? What does this say about their self-esteem?

- Would you rather follow the leadership of someone who is humble or someone who is arrogant? Why?

- "To those whom much has been given, much is expected." Why is this true? What is expected of you?

- How often do you take a moment to reflect on the good things that are happening in your life?

- Is the sharing of these blessings more a duty or more an opportunity? Can it be both?

- How can the tragedies of life be turned around to become a time of positive growth?

STORIES AND THOUGHTS FROM SPIRITUAL TRADITIONS

Hinduism

Therefore I tell you:
Be humble, be harmless,
Have no pretension,
Be upright, forbearing,
Serve your teacher
In true obedience,
Keeping the mind
And the body in cleanness,
Tranquil, steadfast,
Master of ego,
Standing apart
From the things of the senses,
Free from self;
Aware of the weakness
In mortal nature,
Its bondage to birth,
Age, suffering, dying;
To nothing be slave,
Nor desire possession
Of man-child or wife,
Of home or of household;
Calmly encounter
The painful, the pleasant;
Adore me only
With heart undistracted;
Turn all your thought
Toward solitude, spurning
The noise of the crowd,
Its fruitless commotion;
Strive without ceasing
To know the Atman,
Seek this knowledge
And comprehend clearly
Why you should seek it:
Such, it is said,
Are the roots of true wisdom:
Ignorance, merely,
Is all that denies them.

— Bhagavad Gita

A braggart exposes himself to exploitation and downfall. A humble man drinks the nectar of simplicity and the joy of love.

– Tradition

Buddhism

Humility is appreciating that I am one whereas others are many. Where did we ever get the idea that we are more important than others? This grand delusion is the root of all conflicts and problems. My own benefit is the benefit of just one person, while the benefit of others is infinite.

The Tibetans have a saying: we see the faults of others even when they are as small as a flea, but don't see our own faults even when they are as big as an elephant!

Zen Buddhism

When ordinariness and holiness exist no more, how is that? An octagonal grindstone is turning in empty space; a diamond pestle grinds to dust the iron mountain.

Christianity

"Do justice, love kindness and walk humbly with your God."

– Bible, Micah 6:8

"You shall not make for yourself a graven image, or any likeness of anything that is in heaven above."

– Bible, Exodus 20:4

"When pride comes, then comes disgrace; but with the humble is wisdom."

– Bible, Proverbs 11:2

"Pride goes before destruction, and a haughty spirit before a fall."

– Bible, Proverbs 16:18

The Pharisee and the Publican

Jesus told this story to some who boasted of their virtue and looked down on everyone else:

"Two men went to the Temple to pray. One was a proud, self-righteous Pharisee, and the other a cheating tax collector. The proud Pharisee 'prayed' this prayer: 'Thank God, I am not a sinner like everyone else, especially like that tax collector over there! For I never cheat, I don't commit adultery, I go without food twice a week, and I give to God a tenth of everything I earn.'

"But the corrupt tax collector stood at a distance and dared not even lift his eyes to heaven as he prayed, but beat upon his chest in sorrow, exclaiming, 'God, be merciful to me, a sinner.' I tell you, said Jesus, this sinner, not the Pharisee, returned home forgiven! For the proud shall be humbled, but the humble shall be honored."

— Bible, Luke 18:9-14

Islam

The Homa's Excuse

The homa* next addressed the company.
Because his shadow heralds majesty,
This wandering portent of the royal state
Is known as Homayun, 'The Fortunate.'
He sang: 'O birds of land and ocean, I
Am not as other birds, but soar and fly
On lofty aspiration's lordly wings.
I have subdued the dog desire; great kings
Like Feridoun and Jamshid** owe their place
To my dark shadow's influence. Disgrace
And lowly natures are not my concern.
I throw desire its bone; the dog will turn
And let the soul go free. Who can look down
On one whose shadow brings the royal crown?
The world should bask in my magnificence—
Let Khosroe's glory stand in my defence.
What should this haughty Simorgh mean to me?'

The hoopoe said: 'Poor slave to vanity,
Your self-importance is ridiculous;
Why should a shadow merit so much fuss?
You are not now the sign of Khosroe's throne,
More like a stray dog squabbling for a bone.
Though it is true that you confer on men
This majesty, kings must sink down again
And bear the punishments of Judgement Day.'

— The Conference of the Birds p. 43-4

* *A mythical bird whose shadow would fall on a future king.*
** *Two of the most illustrious of the legendary kings of ancient Persia.*

Chinese

"He does not preach what he practices till he has practiced what he preaches."

— Confucius

"To reward merit is to stir up emulation; to display desirable things is to excite the disorder of covetousness."

— Lao Tzu

"Gold and jade endanger the house of their possessor. Wealth and honors lead to arrogance and envy, and bring ruin."

— Lao Tzu

The Master said, He does not mind not being in office; all he minds about is whether he has qualities that entitle him to office. He does not mind failing to get recognition; he is too busy doing the things that entitle him to recognition.

— The Analects, Book IV

Someone said, "Jan Yung is Good, but he is a poor talker." The Master said, "What need has he to be a good talker? Those who down others with clap-trap are seldom popular. Whether he is Good, I do not know. But I see no need for him to be a good talker."

— The Analects, Book V

Heaven and Earth are mighty in continuance, because their work is delivered from the least of result. Thus also the sage, seeking not any goal, attaining all things; he does not interfere in the affairs of the body, and so that body acts without friction. It is because he meddles not with personal aims that these came to pass with simplicity.

— Tao Te Ching

The root of grandeur is humility, and the strength of exaltation is its base. Thus rulers speak of themselves as "Fatherless," "Virtueless," "Unworthy," proclaiming by this that their Glory is in their shame. So also the virtue of a Chariot is not any of the parts of the chariot, if they be numbered. They do not seek to appear fine like jade, but inconspicuous like common stone.

— Tao Te Ching

The Arrogant Azalea and the Humble Pine

Each spring for thousands of years, the Queen of Flowers held a festival to which she invited one hundred of the prettiest flowers. She and all of her guests celebrated the beauty and wonder of spring in the forest.

Once, many years ago, Azalea had been invited, due to her brilliant color and great beauty. She began primping and preparing for the great event, quite certain that she would be the loveliest there. She knew that only the most beautiful flowers would be invited, and even next to them she would be spectacular. Oh, how excited she was! It was all she could think about.

Imagine Azalea's surprise when one day the scraggly little Pine Tree approached and said, "Azalea, dear friend, shall we go together to the Queen's celebration? It would be so much more fun to go with a friend."

Azalea burst into laughter at Pine Tree's suggestion. "Surely you haven't been invited to the festival! You are not even a flower and you are hardly beautiful! In fact, you are small, crooked, and quite homely. There must be some mistake."

Tears ran from Pine Tree's eyes as she tried to sweep them away with one of her branches. "It is true I am not very tall or straight, but I do so love the company of my friends. I am so grateful for the loveliness of spring and for the beauty of all the flowers of the forest. I may not be beautiful, but since the Queen invited me, I will go." Then Pine Tree turned sadly and left Azalea.

"What a bother," said Azalea, ruffling her crimson petals. "It's time now for my beauty sleep." Then Azalea rested her head on her glossy leaves and fell fast asleep.

Meanwhile, Pine Tree made her way slowly to the Queen's festival. Upon her arrival at the gates she was greeted warmly by the Queen of Flowers. A camellia smiled her way and an orchid waved. They were all happy to see the gentle pine tree. She was so happy to be among friends. After all had enjoyed the party for quite some time, the Queen beckoned to Pine Tree. "My dear Pine, I would like to present you with the award for Greatest Beauty."

Quite startled, Pine Tree said, "But I am not a beautiful flower at all."

"Ah, my little friend, you always see the best in others, you find gifts where others find faults, you see the bright side of life. You possess great inner beauty," said the Queen, stroking Pine Tree's young branches.

Just then Azalea arrived, quite indignant at all the attention Pine Tree was receiving. She scowled at Pine Tree, unable to enjoy the celebration and the happiness which surrounded Pine Tree. She gazed on Pine Tree with a hollow, bitter heart. Ever since that moment, Azalea's stems have been hollow as well. Even today, while azaleas continue to be lush and beautiful flowers, they live short lives.

The Pine Tree, however, heartened by friendship and strengthened by love, grew to be very tall and strong, and lived a long and happy life.

Germany

The Modified Horse

Once upon a time, in a small kingdom there lived a sculptor. His beautiful works in stone were appreciated by one and all. Soon his fame spread far and wide. A day came when the king of the land ordered a statue of himself to be done in marble. The humble artist was overjoyed at this royal assignment. He worked hard all day long and well into the midnight hours.

Days passed into weeks and weeks into months. At last, the great work was completed and installed in the public square. The artist had taken great pains to carve the figure of his beloved ruler. On an appointed day, the king rode from his castle, flanked by his favorite courtiers. The statue was unveiled amidst much pomp and show. All stood spellbound! His statue seemed so real that the king was unable to believe that it was made of marble.

"Marvelous! Beautiful! Perfect!" he exclaimed, and turning to the sculptor shook his hands warmly like a good old friend. "You are indeed a great artist! I feel honored that you are one of my subjects. Here, take this sackful of gold as your reward."

But some of the courtiers seethed with jealousy and anger. "We're the king's favorites and his constant companions. But never have we met with such warm affection from him!" they thought to themselves. But they dared not pick any flaws in the statue of their lord, for the king himself had already declared it perfect! What should they do to humiliate their rival?

"Indeed, Your Majesty," began the first one, taking courage, "your marble figure is perfect and we hail the great artist for his skill! But the steed you're mounted upon is not as handsome."

"Yes," joined another, "the figure of the horse is surely out of proportion. Its tail is too long and its head too large."

"The statue of the horse is absolutely a failure. The fall of its mane and the turn of its neck are rather awkward," added the third.

"If only the fold of the horse's left hind leg could be changed, it would stand much smarter," said the fourth.

Thus, one after another, all the jealous courtiers found some fault in the animal's figure. The king nodded to their comments, for they were his counselors. So many of them could not go wrong!

The humble sculptor listened quietly. He then said with a faint smile, "Your Majesty, these honorable men are not very happy with my sculpture of the horse. Allow me seven more days, I shall try to change it to their taste."

The king agreed to his request. The artist ordered temporary curtains to be put over the statue to enable him to work undisturbed. Day in and day out was heard the clang of hammer and chisel. The honorable courtiers did often pass by the enclosure. They were delighted by the sound and chuckled, looking at one another meaningfully.

Soon the seven long days passed, and the people who lived nearby gave a sigh of relief. For the loud noise of hammer and chisel had at last stopped. All gathered in the central square. The king arrived, flanked by his favorite courtiers. The screens were drawn and the statue was unveiled once again.

The ruler exclaimed at its beauty and beamed a smile at its creator. The sculptor looked at his first critic and said, "Revered sir, your comment was so much to the point that I devoted two full days to modify the figure accordingly. How do you find it now?"

The artist then turned to one after another of all his critics and praised them for their high aesthetic sense, asking them if they were satisfied with the modified horse. Indeed, they were thoroughly satisfied!

"Perfect!" said the eldest of the courtiers. "The steed is the most handsome that I have ever set my eyes upon."

"Yes, the work is now finely proportioned, with the animal's elegant head, and its tail not too long," said the second earnestly.

"How graceful are the fall of its mane and the turn of its neck!" exclaimed the other.

"Much smarter is the position of the horse's rear left leg. Indeed, it enhances the beauty of the work now!" said the fourth, pretending to be one with the fine aesthetic taste in the court.

"O sculptor," said the king at last, "all my courtiers are happy with your creation. They think that it is now perfect, after you have improved upon it according to their suggestions."

But the modest man smiled and replied in a measured tone, "Your Majesty, I'm indeed fortunate to have such great and educated critics of art. But alas, the fact is, I have changed nothing. The work is as it was when you first saw it."

All stood amazed, once staring at the great statue and then at its creator.

"What do you mean? Didn't we hear the sound of your tools?" asked the king, rather surprised.

"O Lord, indeed you heard the sound of chisel and the hammer. I was only hammering at the virtuous quality of your loyal courtiers, who found faults in my work simply because they were jealous," explained the sculptor with a low bow.

The king turned towards his men. They stood, heads hung.

"Bravo, my dear good man! Bravo!" exclaimed the king, affectionately patting the sculptor on the back. "You've not only created a marvelous piece of art but also hammered my courtiers' pride and reputation to pieces!"

Japanese

The Stonecutter

Once, long ago, there was a humble stonecutter named Tasaku. Each morning he rose early to go to work at the base of a mountain where he chipped away the stone with his hammer and chisel. Every day, he was content to carve the great blocks of stone from which beautiful palaces and temples would be built. He was very happy with his task and asked for nothing more. Tasaku's good and simple outlook made the Spirit of the Mountain very happy, and the Spirit was pleased by Tasaku's kind nature.

But one day, as Tasaku was busy with his hammer and chisel, a great and beautiful procession passed by. First, there came a large army of proud soldiers. Then Tasaku saw a fine prince who was dressed in splendor and carried aloft by many servants. There were lovely dancers and musicians parading behind. Tasaku watched the magnificent stream of people with awe until they moved out of sight.

After witnessing such splendor and the prince in all his finery, Tasaku could not bring himself to return to his humble work. He no longer wanted to spend his life at the base of the mountain cutting stone. He envied the prince. His heart longed for a life of wealth and power. The Spirit of the Mountain heard the desires of his heart and, that very night, transformed the lowly stonecutter into a fine prince.

Tasaku awoke the next morning in a beautiful palace surrounded by servants ready to do his bidding. He wore magnificent robes of the finest silk, and dancers moved before him while musicians played for his enjoyment. He was overjoyed with his new life.

Each day he would stroll in his garden, enjoying the lovely blossoms and fruit trees. One day, he sought shelter from the heat of the sun beneath the branches of a tree, and he noticed that the sun's searing rays had withered some of his precious blooms. He thought about the great power of the sun and became discontent. The sun's power was far greater than that of a prince. Tasaku longed to be as powerful as the sun!

Once again, the Spirit of the Mountain heard Tasaku's desires and transformed him instantly into the sun. The feeling of such power thrilled Tasaku. He shone so brightly and proudly in the sky that it was not long before he scorched fields and burned crops. His strong rays began to dry the lands and the people became desperate for water.

At long last, a large group of clouds came over Tasaku and covered his rays completely. Tasaku then realized that the clouds were even more powerful than the sun. Once more, he became discontent and longed to become a great cloud. The Spirit of the Mountain heard his wishes and transformed him into an enormous cloud.

Haughtily, Tasaku puffed himself up and began to rain powerfully over the land. Proud of his new strength, he sent huge storms over the fields. He flooded fields and homes in his excitement, and finally even temples and palaces were washed away. All was gone, destroyed by his power. All but the mountain.

Tasaku was enraged by the immovable mountain. Angry that the mountain was more powerful than the cloud, he cried out, "Turn me into the mountain!" Without hesitating, the Spirit did so and departed, knowing that there was nothing more that he could do to please Tasaku.

So all at once, Tasaku became the mountain. At last, he thought, he was more magnificent than the prince, more powerful than the sun, and far stronger than the cloud. He stood there so proudly. Finally, he was greater than everything around him.

Suddenly, he felt a sharp pain at his feet. It was the sting of a chisel! There, far below, was a lowly stonecutter, hammering slowly but surely at his base.

While bits of stone cracked and crumbled from him, so did Tasaku's heart.

PROVERBS AND MAXIMS

Great character has no facades. It shines with honesty, respect, true humility, and an inner faith that knows we are but the recipients of a great gift.

– T. Pagna

Life is a long lesson in humility.

– Barrie

If you compare yourself to others, you may become vain and bitter; for always there will be greater and lesser persons than yourself.

– Desiderata

If the only prayer you say in your whole life is "thank you," that would suffice.

– M. Eckhart

A hundred times a day I remind myself that my inner and outer life depends on the labors of other men, living and dead, and that I must exert myself in order to give in the measure as I have received and am still receiving.

– A. Einstein

HEROES AND HEROINES

SACAGAWEA (1786–?)

Born in territory which is now part of Idaho, she was of the Shoshone tribe of Native Americans, but was captured by an enemy tribe and sold to the Missouri River Mandans. She married a French Canadian fur trader who lived in the Mandan village. When Meriwether Lewis and William Clark appeared on the river in 1804 on their way west, her husband was hired as an interpreter for the expedition and Sacagawea was allowed to accompany him. Her abilities as a guide, interpreter, and diplomatic liaison with other tribes proved invaluable to Lewis and Clark. Nothing is known of her life after the expedition ended in 1812, but she is remembered for her courage, her love of adventure, and her loyalty to family and friends.

MARY MCLEOD BETHUNE (1875–1955)

Born in Mayesville, South Carolina, she was the daughter of former slaves, who had seventeen children; Mary was the fifteenth. She was raised on a farm and educated in a Presbyterian mission school. While she had a serious mind, she still enjoyed music and dance, and was an acknowledged leader of her classmates. She graduated from the Moody Bible Institute and, unable to pursue her desire to become a missionary in Africa, became a teacher. She opened a school for African-American girls in Daytona Beach, Florida in 1904. The school survived, merged with a boys' school, and eventually became Bethune-Cookman College. In 1936, President Franklin Roosevelt appointed her director of African-American affairs in the National Youth Administration. She is recognized as one of America's great educators, an advisor to several American presidents, and a powerful champion of racial equality.

JIMMY CARTER (1924–)

Born in Plains, Georgia, as James Earl Carter, he was the 39th president of the United States from 1977–1981. Of humble birth, he was the son of a farmer and a nurse; he listed his occupation as a peanut farmer and warehouseman. He was the first president to use his nickname at his inauguration and the first one to walk from the Capitol to the White House afterward. His administration was characterized by a human rights policy that he considered an integral factor in the relationship between the United States and other countries. Following his term as president, he remained active in a local Baptist church as a Sunday school teacher, worked as a volunteer for Habitat for Humanity, and represented the United States as a peacemaker in several trouble spots around the world.

MOHANDAS GANDHI (1869–1948)

Born in Porbandar, India, into a wealthy family of the Vaisya, or merchant caste, he was a small, quiet boy who disliked sports and was only an average student. He wanted to study medicine but was prevailed upon by his father to study law. His belief in non-violence was fostered by racial discrimination and violence in South Africa, by a reading of Thoreau's essay on "Civil Disobedience," by correspondence with Leo Tolstoy, and by reading John Rushin's *Unto this Last*. He became a vegetarian, took voluntary vows of poverty and chastity, and created a cooperative commonwealth for civil resistors called the Tolstoy Farm. He devoted his life to Indian independence from England, equal justice for all of the people of India, and unity between Hindus and Moslems. While attending prayers, he was shot and killed by a Hindu extremist.

*H*umility ————————————————————————————— EMBRACING

PUT HUMILITY INTO ACTION

- Be part of the group, not the star of the show; share the credit.

- Be strong in character and gentle in criticism.

- Find ways to express your thankfulness to the people who have contributed to your happiness.

- Contribute to someone else's happiness.

- Get involved in a community service project and participate regularly.

- Praise the accomplishments of others, and speak sparingly of your own (only when asked).

- When in a position of leadership, lead by example and with polite requests.

- Make a list of the things that are expected of you.

- Take a few minutes each day for quiet reflection.

- Create a habit of verbal thank yous and writing thank you notes.

COMMUNITY SERVICE IDEAS

- Volunteer to serve food in a homeless shelter.

- Make placemats and/or placecards for an annual Thanksgiving dinner for the disadvantaged.

- Write a letter thanking the people who clean your classroom; have everyone in the class sign it.

- Volunteer at an elderly healthcare center; visit elderly patients and help with arts and crafts, exercise programs, and other activities.

- Volunteer to read to pre-school children in a daycare center or children's hospital.

- Bake cookies and/or make greeting cards for shut-ins.

BOOKS ON HUMILITY

A Chair for My Mother. Vera Williams. New York: Greenwillow Books, 1982.

Raven. Gerald McDermott. San Diego: Harcourt Brace, Jovanovich, 1993.

Sylvester and the Magic Pebble. William Steig. New York: Simon, 1969.

A Call to Character. Colin Greer and Herbert Kohl, eds. New York:
Harper Collins Publisher, 1995.

"The Head Man" – p. 72

"Narrative of the Life of Frederick Douglass, An American Slave" – p. 74

"Simple Gifts" – p. 69

Chicken Soup for the Teenage Soul. Jack Canfield, et al. Deerfield Beach: Health
Communications, Inc., 1997.

"What is Success?" – p. 248

The Moral Compass. William J. Bennett, ed. New York: Simon and Schuster, 1995.

"The Golden Tripod" – p. 729

"A Little Learning" – p. 734

"Robert of Sicily" – p. 725

"Saint Augustine by the Seashore" – p. 744

December

Peace

SUPPORTIVE VALUES

Harmony • Forgiveness

DEFINITIONS

A state of tranquility, harmony in relationships.

There is an outer **peace** and an inner peace. There is the peace which refers to communities where there is no violence and everyone is able to live a fulfilled life. There is a peace which refers to self, where security and self-worth enable a person to feel at peace with oneself. These are the kinds of peace which we are referring to in this month's value.

Harmony is a word usually coupled with peace. It is also used in terms of musical harmony, where many voices or instruments play different melodies which create more depth and beauty in the composition.

Forgiveness is ceasing the feeling of resentment towards someone who has offended or hurt you in any way.

PURPOSE

We are aware of the state of unrest in our world; there are wars in many countries as well as increased violence in our own cities. We look outward, and forget that if we truly desire peace on earth it needs to begin with each one of us. Our actions toward ourselves and those around us speak clearly about the degree to which we are at peace with ourselves. Inner peace is a good place to start. Spinoza explains, "Peace is not an absence of war, it is a virtue, a state of mind, a disposition for benevolence, confidence, justice."

Horace wrote, "It is right for him who asks forgiveness for his offenses to grant it to others." We always hope for forgiveness but often have difficulty giving it when we feel we've been wronged. When we learn to forgive ourselves, we are more forgiving of others. An inability to forgive, bearing a grudge for some past hurt, is an obstacle on the path to inner peace. As teachers, we need to strive to be forgiving of our students if we expect them to be forgiving of each other and of us, for we sometimes need our students' forgiveness to help us find our own inner peace.

Peace

Day One:
Without discussing it with anyone, write your own definition of peace. Then compare and contrast definitions from various members of the class.

Day Two:
Discuss the meaning of peace using the definitions on page 71 and those written yesterday. Is peace hard to define?

Day Three:
In small groups, use the discussion questions on page 74 as a springboard for developing ten more questions related to peace.

Day Four:
What symbols can you think of which represent peace? Make the most exhaustive a list you can.

Day Five:
Create a banner for peace to hang up outside your classroom. Be sure to decorate it with several symbols of peace from yesterday's list.

Day Six:
When problems arise—a peaceful solution is preferable for all involved. Why? Write down the criteria for finding a peaceful solution.

Day Seven:
Make a bookmark from a proverb on page 81. Keep it in a special book as a reminder of peace as a value to be treasured.

Day Eight:
Find out about the history and purpose of the Nobel Peace Prize. Research and learn about one Nobel prize winner. Write a one page essay on what this person did to receive such a highly esteemed award.

Day Nine:
If your school had an annual award comparable to the Nobel Peace Prize, who would you nominate to win the prize? Prepare a brief paragraph to support your candidate's nomination. Be specific as to the person's qualifications.

Day Ten:
Consider what you would do if someone who did not value peace tried to fight with you or mistreats you. Share your ideas in a small group and as a group decide on the best resolution to the problem.

Day Eleven:
In a total class setting, share and discuss the problems and suggestions for resolution from yesterday.

Day Twelve:
During the Civil Rights Movement in America many Americans fought civil injustice through peaceful demonstrations. These people are extraordinary examples of those who truly value peace. Use reference materials to learn about these demonstrators and their influences.

Day Thirteen:
Write a journal entry about the power of peace.

Day Fourteen:
How can you promote peace in your own life? Make a list of peaceful acts which you can do today. Choose one and act and follow through to promote peace.

Day Fifteen:
Create a petition for students and their teachers to sign—pledging their support for peace and committing to promote peace in their own environment and around the world. Be sure to give everyone in your school an opportunity to sign the pledge.

Day Sixteen:
How would the world today be different if there were world peace? Write a short story about life in a peaceful world.

Day Seventeen:
Make lists of things people of your age can do to promote peace in your community, in your country, and in the world. How are the three lists alike and different?

Day Eighteen:
History is filled with examples of non-peaceful periods. Reflect on one period in particular. Write your thoughts in a journal entry about what caused peace to be forfeited and of the consequences of this forfeiture.

Day Nineteen:
Name and define ways education contributes to world peace. Discuss why and how educated people can promote peace for people with less education.

Day Twenty:
Review what you have learned about peace this month and reflect on how you can embrace peace on a daily basis.

PEACE IN OTHER LANGUAGES

Chinese   *ping*   level; even; just; equal; average; ordinary; common

                an   quiet; still; peace; tranquility

French   *la paix*   state of concord, agreement among members of a group or nations; tranquility; lack of noise, agitation, disorder; serenity of mind

German   *friede*   peace, tranquility

Hawaiian   *maluhia*   peace, quiet, tranquility, serenity

Japanese   *heiwa*   quiet harmony
                                hei—flat
                                wa—harmony

Korean   *pyung hwa*   evenly harmonized; reconciliation

Latin   *pax*   peace

Spanish   *paz*   peace

Tagalog   *kapayapaan*   freedom from war or strife; a public quiet, order and security

DISCUSSION QUESTIONS

• In a song we sing are the words, "Let there be peace on earth, and let it begin with me." How is this possible?

• Is there a situation where you have forgiven someone? Did it establish a kind of peace?

• Describe a time when you are at complete peace.

• When people are striving for harmony during a disagreement, are they suggesting people change their minds, or that they try to understand the other's position?

• Martin Luther King, Jr. said, "Peace is not just the absence of war. It is the presence of understanding and acceptance." Do you agree? Why or why not?

• Why is it hard to forgive someone who has harmed us? Why is it so important and so necessary?

• Can the same principles and procedures for peace in our personal relationships be transferred to nations?

• Describe your most peaceful moment.

STORIES AND THOUGHTS FROM SPIRITUAL TRADITIONS

Hinduism

No Hope in Killing Kinsmen

Then Krishna, subduer of the senses, thus requested by Arjuna, the conqueror of sloth, drove that most splendid of chariots into a place between the two armies, confronting Bhisma, Drona and all those other rulers of the earth. And he said: 'O Prince, behold the assembled Kurus!'

Then the prince, Arjuna, looked on the array, and in both armies he recognized fathers and grandfathers, teachers, uncles, sons, brothers, grandsons, fathers-in-law, dear friends, and many other familiar faces.

When Arjuna saw all those ranks of kinsmen, he was filled with deep compassion, and he spoke despairingly, as follows:

Arjuna:

Krishna, Krishna,
Now as I look on
These my kinsmen
Arrayed for battle,
My limbs are weakened,
My mouth is parching,
My body trembles,
My hair stands upright,
My skin seems burning,
The bow Gandiva
Slips from my hand,
My brain is whirling
Round and round,
I can stand no longer:
Krishna, I see such
Omens of evil!
What can we hope from
This killing of kinsmen?

Knower of all things,
Though they should slay me
How could I harm them?
I cannot wish it:
Never, never,
Not though it won me
The throne of the three worlds;
How much the less for
Earthly lordship!

Rather than this
Let the evil children
Of Dhritarashtra
Come with their weapons
Against me in battle:
I shall not struggle,
I shall not strike them.
Now let them kill me,
That will be better.

– Bhagavad Gita

Peace can be reached by concentrating on that which is dearest to the heart.
– Sivananda

When one goes beyond the duality of the external world, then one finds true peace, for it exists alone within.

– Upanishads

Lust, anger, pride, and greed, all lead to rebirth in a hell realm. The true peace comes in removing these from one's heart and replacing them with love of God.

– Ramcaritmanas

The noblest vengeance is forgiveness.

– Tradition

Buddhism

The key to world peace is creating peace within our own hearts.

Christianity

"Glory to God in the highest, and on earth, peace and goodwill among all people."

– Bible, Luke 2:14

"You shall not kill."

– Bible, Exodus 20:13

"Live in harmony with one another. Repay no one evil for evil. Live peaceably with all."

– Bible, Romans 12:16-18.

Love your Enemies (A Portion from The Sermon on the Mount)

"The law of Moses says, 'If a man gouges out another's eye, he must pay with his own eye. If a tooth gets knocked out, knock out the tooth of the one who did it.' But I say: Don't resist violence! If you are slapped on one cheek, turn the other too. If you are ordered to go to court, and your shirt is taken from you, give your coat too. If the military demand that you carry their gear for a mile, carry it two. Give to those who ask, and don't turn away from those who want to borrow.

There is a saying, 'Love your friends and hate your enemies.' But I say: Love your enemies! Pray for those who persecute you! In that way you will be acting as true sons of your Father in heaven. For he gives his sunlight to both the evil and the good, and sends rain on the just and on the unjust too. If you love only those who love you, what good is that? Even scoundrels do that much. If you are friendly only to your friends, how are you different from anyone else? Even the heathen do that. But you are to be perfect, even as your Father in heaven is perfect."

– Bible, Matthew 5:38-48

Islam

'Ali, the "Lion of God," was once engaged in conflict with a Magian chief, and in the midst of the struggles the Magian spat in his face. 'Ali, instead of taking vengeance on him, at once dropped his sword, to the Magian's great astonishment. On his inquiring the reason of such forbearance, 'Ali informed him that the "Lion of God" did not destroy life for the satisfaction of his own vengeance, but simply to carry out God's will, and that whenever he saw just cause, he held his hand even in the midst of the strife, and spared the foe. The Prophet, 'Ali continued, had long since informed him that he would die by the hand of his own stirrup-bearer (Ibn Maljun), and the stirrup-bearer had frequently implored 'Ali to kill him, and

Character Education Year 2 Grades 6–12

thus save him from the commission of that great crime; but 'Ali said he always refused to do so, as to him death was as sweet as life, and he felt no anger against his destined assassin, who was only the instrument of God's eternal purpose. The Magian chief, on hearing 'Ali's discourse, was so much affected that he embraced Islam, together with all his family, to the number of fifty souls.

[A clarification of the above story is that the Magian chief is unarmed when he spits on 'Ali. Therefore, 'Ali reveals self-control by not striking.]

['Ali will not strike the Magian chief out of vengeance. He also will not kill his stirrup-bearer to preserve his own life. Displaying an internal peace, 'Ali views death "as sweet as life." In other words, he not only restrains from unnecessary violence, but is at peace with himself and prepared to meet God. This story illustrates that Islam promotes peace. The only reason for warfare or killing is "God's will."]

– Teachings of Rumi p56-7
Story XVI. 'Ali's Forbearance (p.92)

I found this inscribed on the hilt of the Prophet's sword: 'Forgive him who wrongs thee; join him who cuts thee off; do good to him who does evil to thee, and speak the truth although it be against thyself.'

– Selections from Mishkat-ul-masabi [243] p. 56
'Aliy, RA

Blessed is he who is guided to Islam, and whose livelihood is daily bread, and who is contented.

– Selections from Mishkat-ul-masabi [126] p. 32 Fudalah b. Ubayd, TI

But if the enemy inclines towards peace, then you should also incline towards peace, and trust in Allah, for He is the One that hears and knows all.

Should they intend to deceive you—truly Allah is sufficient to you. It is He who strengthens you with His Aid and with the Believers.

The root of the word Islam means, amongst other things, Peace. To incline towards peace is to incline towards Allah. War is at times an unavoidable step to peace. It is the price we pay for free will, for it is the ultimate expression of conflicting wills. But whenever there is a possibility of peace with our enemies we should take it, rather than continue fighting out of fear or suspicion. If, indeed, it is a trick by our enemies, then Allah and the solidarity He has given us amongst ourselves will come to our aid.

– Selections from Mishkat-ul-masabi [253] p. 164
Spoils of War (Anfal) 8:61

Chinese

"If out of the three hundred songs I had to take one phrase to cover all my teaching, I would say, Let there be no evil in your thoughts."   – *Confucius*

"Never do to others what you would not like them to do to you."
                                                                – *Confucius*

"Let us make our sharpness blunt; let us loosen our complexes; let us tone down our brightness to the general obscurity."   – *Lao Tzu*

"Who can clear muddy water? Stillness will accomplish this. Who can obtain rest? Let motion continue equably, and it will itself be peace."
                                                                – *Lao Tzu*

"Where armies are, are weeds. Bad harvests follow great hosts."   – *Lao Tzu*

When Master Tseng was ill, Meng Ching Tzu came to see him. Master Tseng spoke to him saying, When a bird is about to die, its song touches the heart. When a man is about to die, his words are of note. There are three things that a gentleman, in following the Way, places above all the rest: from every attitude, every gesture that he employs he must remove all trace of violence or arrogance; every look that he composes in his face must betoken good faith; from every word that he utters, from every intonation, he must remove all trace of coarseness or impropriety.   – *The Analects, Book VIII*

The Master said, To have faults and to be making no effort to amend them is to have faults indeed! A man can enlarge his Way; but there is no Way that can enlarge a man. He whose wisdom brings him into power, needs Goodness to secure that power. Else, though he get it, he will certainly lose it. He whose wisdom brings him into power and who has Goodness whereby to secure that power, if he has not dignity wherewith to approach the common people, they will not respect him.   – *The Analects, Book XV*

Admire the High Way of Water! Is not Water the soul of the life of things, whereby they change? Yet it seeks its level and abides content in obscurity. So also it resembles the Tao.

The virtue of a house is to be well-placed; of the mind, to be at ease in silence as of Space; of societies, to be well-disposed; of government, to maintain quietude; of work, to be skillfully performed; and of all motion, to be made at the right time.

Also it is the virtue of a man to abide in his place without discontent; thus he offends no man.   – *Tao Te Ching*

India

Character Certificate

Kumar was the son of a farmer. He approached Ramanath, a rich trader, who was looking for an assistant. Ramanath told Kumar he would give him a job provided Kumar gave a security deposit of a thousand rupees. "Alternatively, you may ask four prominent persons to stand surety for you. I'm wary of employing strangers," he told Kumar pointblank.

"All right," agreed Kumar. "If you'll go with me in the evening after you close your shop, I shall get you a thousand rupees or four sureties."

Late in the evening, Kumar took Ramanath to moneylender Vairabh. He told the moneylender the purpose of his visit. "Kumar, you're honest and good," said Vairabh in the presence of Ramanath. "You're not given to telling lies. All this I know well, and I know for certain, too. But, I can't give you a loan. How'll you return the amount? I know your financial status. So, please don't press me for a loan."

Kumar then took Ramanath to Muthuswami, who was a prominent figure of that town. He listened to the youngster's pleas. "I know you even from your childhood; you're also the son of my best friend. You don't quarrel with others for anything and everything; you're also honest. But all that will not prompt me to give you a thousand rupees—as a loan or a gift. I hope you won't insist or bother me again and again."

Kumar's next visit was to the village chief Manikyam. "Look here! I know everybody in your family, Kumar. I also know you well—that you're clever, competent, honest, and won't cheat. But all that will not be sufficient for me to stand surety for you, my boy!"

Kumar was disappointed. He came out and told Ramanath, "See how difficult it is to get a loan. It's all my misfortune!"

"Don't worry, Kumar," Ramanath consoled him. "The certificates of surety I wanted you to get me, I've already received. I don't need them in writing any longer. I've heard all of them describing you and your honesty. That's more than sufficient. You may join my company tomorrow."

Kumar was happy. Though no one was willing to give him a loan of a thousand rupees, it was not a reflection on his character. They did not want to help him with money. At the same time, they all spoke highly of his character. That was enough for Ramanath to assess Kumar. More than a surety certificate, what he wanted was a character certificate.

PROVERBS AND MAXIMS

Go placidly amid the noise and haste, and remember what peace there may be in silence . . . be at peace with God, whatever you conceive Him to be, and whatever your labors and aspirations, in the noisy confusion of life keep peace with your soul.

— *Desiderata*

**Peace is not an absence of war,
it is a virtue, a state of mind, a disposition
for benevolence, confidence, justice.**

— *Spinoza*

Be always the first, do not wait for others to forgive.
For by forgiving you become the master of fate, the fashioner of life, the doer of miracles.
To forgive is the highest, most beautiful form of love.
In return you will receive untold peace and happiness.

— *Mueller*

To err is human, to forgive, divine.

— *Pope*

**If the pursuit of peace is both old and new, it is also both
complicated and simple. It is complicated, for it has to do
with people, and nothing in this universe baffles man
as much as man himself.**

— *Stevenson*

HEROES AND HEROINES

MADELINE KORBEL ALBRIGHT (1937–)

Born in Prague, Czechoslovakia, she moved to London when she was two years old and to America in 1948. She attended Wellesley College, graduating with honors and a degree in political science in 1959. She married Joseph Albright, a newspaper reporter, a few days after graduation. She enrolled in graduate school at Columbia University, eventually earning a masters and Ph.D. At the same time she was working for Senator Edmund Muskie, and in 1978 joined the staff of the National Security Council under Zbigniew Brezejinski, who was President Jimmy Carter's national security advisor. She has served as the United States permanent representative to the United Nations since 1993. She has acted not only as a spokesperson for the executive arm of the government but as a significant behind-the-scenes strategist and policy-maker. She has earned a reputation as an expert in foreign policy and has already made significant contributions as an advocate for peace.

RIGOBERTA MENCHU (1959–)

Born in the village of Chimel in northwestern Guatemala, she is a member of the Quiche, one of twenty-two groups of Mayan Indians. By age eight she was toiling on the coffee plantations under conditions that approximated slavery. Her family's efforts to improve conditions and to resist the Guatemalan soldiers from taking their land resulted in the torture and killing of her father, mother and younger brother during 1979 and 1980. In 1981 she escaped to Mexico, where she has lived in exile ever since. She continues to speak out for justice and a peaceful resolution in Guatemala. She yearns for a normal life of family and peace, but repeated death threats keep her "homeless" and in isolation. She was awarded the Nobel Peace Prize in 1992.

YITZHAK RABIN (1922–1995)

Born in Jerusalem of Russian parents, who moved to Palestine during World War I, Yitzhak received his education in Tel Aviv and in a kibbutz. He planned to become a pioneer farmer, but World War II interrupted his studies in Berkeley, and he joined the Pulmach, the highly trained commando force of the Haganah. By 1964 he had achieved the rank of Major General in the Israeli army. Upon retirement from the military he became ambassador to the United States and entered Israeli politics. A military hero who evolved into a peacemaker, he became Prime Minister of Israel and negotiated several peace accords with Yasir Arafat of the PLO. He shared the Nobel Peace Prize with Arafat and Israeli defense minister Shimon Peres. While leaving a Tel Aviv "Peace Now" rally, at which he had just spoken, he was shot to death by a right-wing Israeli Jew.

EMBRACING

ANWAR SADAT (1918–1981)

Born in a Nile delta village in Egypt, he was one of thirteen children in a devoutly Moslem family. He studied the Koran in a local religious school and in 1925 his family moved to Cairo, where he went to high school. He developed a passion for ending the British influence in Egypt and became a military officer. He continued his work for the freedom of Egypt and became President of the United Arab Republic in 1970. When the conflict between Egypt and Israel worsened, he worked with Israeli Prime Minister Menachem Begin to restore peace. In 1978 he and Begin were awarded the Nobel Peace Prize.

DESMOND TUTU (1931–)

Born in the gold-mining town of Klerkadorp, South Africa, he moved with his family to Johannesburg, where he attended high school and college. He taught in a high school from 1954–1957 but decided to enter the ministry of the Anglican Church when the government instituted an inferior system for blacks. This change coincided with political developments in South Africa and the beginning of the anti-apartheid movement. He became a leader of the South African Council of Churches and a voice of moderation in the struggle against apartheid. His work resulted in his being awarded the Nobel Peace Prize in 1984. He continues to express his belief that "there is no peace because there is no justice. We are struggling not to oppress somebody else but in order to free everybody."

ELIE WIESEL (1928–)

Born in Sighet, Rumania, he was raised within the Hasidic Jewish tradition by his parents, who fostered in him the importance of the Hasidic spirit, studying and living a life that was devoted to God. When the Nazis occupied Rumania in 1944 his family was sent to the Birkenau concentration camp, where his father died of starvation and his mother and younger sister perished in the gas chambers. In 1945 he was transferred to Buchenwald, where he was liberated in April of that year. He studied philosophy in an effort to understand the horrors he had experienced, and became a journalist, traveling widely while trying to learn and write about human suffering. It was ten years before he could write about his encounter with the evil of the concentration camps. His subsequent writing, teaching, and lecturing on behalf of the victims of violence everywhere led to his being awarded the Nobel Peace Prize in 1986.

PUT PEACE INTO ACTION

- Make peace with someone you have disagreed with.

- When someone apologizes, accept it gratefully and sincerely.

- Find a time, every day, when you can have a few minutes of peace.

- Think of someone you disagree with, and figure out a way to understand and accept them.

- Seek out someone against whom you hold a grudge and forgive them.

- Contact Amnesty International and write a letter asking for the release of a prisoner of conscience.

- Considering musical harmony as a metaphor, how can the different cultures, religions, races, political systems, etc. of the world create a harmonious global family?

COMMUNITY SERVICE IDEAS

- Volunteer to be trained as a peer-mediator through the Neighborhood Justice Center.

- Volunteer with a Peace Education Program.

- Organize Christmas caroling for a hospital.

- Volunteer with a center that prevents child abuse.

- Collect toiletries, toys, and clothes for a shelter for abused spouses.

- Invite a local law enforcement officer to your classroom to talk about ways to promote a peaceful community environment.

BOOKS ON PEACE

Billy the Great. Rosa Gui. New York: Doubleday Books for Young Readers, 1992.
Butter Battle Book. Dr. Seuss. New York: Random House, 1984.
Island of the Skog. Steven Kellogg. New York: Dial Press, 1973.
Smoky Night. Eve Bunting. San Diego: Harcourt Brace, 1994.
Teammates. Peter Golenboch. San Diego: Harcourt Brace, Jovanovich, 1990.

The Book of Virtues. William J. Bennett, ed. New York: Simon and Schuster, 1993.
    "Bausis and Philemon" – p. 303
    "The Enchanted Bluff" – p. 320
    "Jonathan and David" – p. 299
    "Mending Wall" – p. 338
    "Ruth and Naomi" – p. 296
    "A Wayfaring Song" – p. 312

Patience

SUPPORTIVE VALUES

Perseverance • Confidence

DEFINITIONS

Being able to bear difficulties calmly and without complaint.

One definition of **patience** is "steadfast despite opposition, difficulty, or adversity." The capacity for calmly waiting; for ideas, for growth, for achievement, regardless of obstacles in our path, is patience. *Ahonui,* the Hawaiian word for patience, literally means "large breath," something we need to do (inhale deeply) when we're struggling with our patience. *Ho'omanawanui* is another Hawaiian word for patience which literally means "to make time large," an interesting perspective for looking at the concept of time in regard to patience.

Another word for **perseverance** is persistence. The idea of continuing or persisting in a certain action or on a specific course in spite of any deterrent describes the value of perseverance.

Confidence stresses faith in oneself and one's talents without any suggestion of conceit or arrogance.

PURPOSE

In an age where instant gratification is the norm, it is understandable that students expect immediate results. In lives that are so goal and schedule oriented, patience is a virtue which sometimes seems beyond our grasp. Impatience is often accepted as a natural characteristic of youth, yet as we mature and experience life, we realize that the greatest human achievements in our world all required patience, perseverance, and confidence. When we are patient with ourselves and others we are able to persevere in any situation. When we are confident about our abilities we are aware that it is just a matter of patience and perseverance before we will succeed in our goals.

As educators teach and interact with students, they strive to demonstrate that being patient, although not always easy, is necessary, not only in regard to achievement but especially in regard to relationships and building character.

Patience

Day One:
Use the definitions on page 87 as a springboard to discuss the meaning of patience.

Day Two:
Why is it sometimes difficult for people of your age to demonstrate patience? Think of ways to help an impatient person become more patient.

Day Three:
Choose one of the bookmarks on page 99 to use to remind you to be patient with yourself and others every day.

Day Four:
Read a story about patience from pages 91–98. Discuss the consequences of impatience.

Day Five:
Remember a time when you had to be patient for something. Write a short story about your experience. Was being patient worth the reward in the end?

Day Six:
Patience requires a good amount of self-control. Practice your capacity for patience by trying as a class to be completely still and quiet for ten minutes. Follow up with a discussion of why some students found it difficult to be patient.

Day Seven:
Remembering your exercise in patience yesterday—collaborate to recommend tips for being patient to help those who had a tough time exercising patience.

Day Eight:
Integrate your list of suggestions from yesterday into a chart to display in your classroom, so that students may refer to it whenever they find a lack of patience. Students might then make their own copy to take home and display.

Day Nine:
Read about the heroes and heroines of patience on pages 100–102. Do you think you could have exercised the same patience that they did? What can you learn from these people about the rewards of patience?

Day Ten:
Make a plan to teach a math or spelling lesson to a younger student. Remember to be a patient teacher!

Day Eleven:
Have you ever had a difficult time learning something? Do you remember the teacher or parent who patiently took the time to help you? Write that person a letter thanking him or her for their patience with you.

Day Twelve:
Patience is like a muscle. To be patient more easily, you must practice using your "patient muscle." Where do you think a patient muscle would be in your body? What do you think it would look like? Draw a picture and share your idea with the class.

Day Thirteen:
List some activities that you do which require patience. Choose one activity where you could be more patient. Write a journal entry about how you will become more patient.

Day Fourteen:
Why is it as important to be patient with yourself as it is to be patient with others. Frustration is a feeling you can get when you are impatient with yourself. Write a brief paragraph about what you will say to yourself when you feel yourself becoming frustrated, and don't forget your own good advice!

Day Fifteen:
Do you think patience is an inherited trait or that people learn to be patient just as they learn to walk, talk, or develop sports skills? Justify your answer.

Day Sixteen:
Make a list of words synonymous with patience (for example, perseverance). Use a dictionary and/or thesaurus for help.

Day Seventeen:
Use one of the following story starters to write a creative story: "The trouble all started with the impatient teenager's lack of self-control . . ." —"The king's patience was sorely tested . . ." —"The referee at last Saturday's soccer game tried hard to be patient but . . ."

Day Eighteen:
Interview someone who demonstrates extreme patience in his or her daily activities to find out how they developed this behavior. Write a character sketch describing this person.

Day Nineteen:
Reflect back to day thirteen. Re-read the journal entry you wrote on that day. Have you embraced patience as you planned? Write in your journal about your success or failure.

Day Twenty:
Review what you have learned about patience this month. Determine if patience is a value worth embracing and what you can do right now to become a more patient person.

LEARNING ABOUT ———————————————————

PATIENCE IN OTHER LANGUAGES

Chinese	*ren*	to endure; to bear; to repress; to forbear
French	*la patience*	aptitude for enduring with constancy or resignation the problems or unpleasant aspects of existence; characteristic of someone who can wait or persevere without irritation or fatigue
Hawaiian	*ahonui*	patient, enduring (aho means "breath, to breathe" and nui means "big, large, great")
Japanese	*nin*	blade on your heart
Korean	*in rae*	patiently persevere, tolerance
Latin	*patientia*	from Latin "pati" (to suffer, endure) (enduring suffering)
Spanish	*paciencia*	patience, forbearance
Tagalog	*tiyaga*	steady effort and perseverance to accomplish a task or responsibility

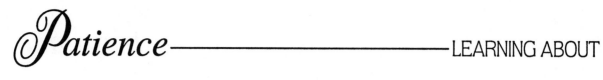

DISCUSSION QUESTIONS

• What or who makes you lose your patience? How could you develop more patience?

• Why are patient people easy to get along with?

• When or how are you confident?

• Is there a limit to how long one should be patient?

• What personality traits or values enable one to be patient?

• How can you develop or improve your perseverance?

• Have you ever been tempted to quit in the midst of a difficult task? What helped you keep going?

• How could you help a classmate deal with his or her impatience?

• How do you remember to be patient in frustrating situations?

STORIES AND THOUGHTS FROM SPIRITUAL TRADITIONS

Hinduism

Patiently, little by little, a man must free himself from all mental distractions, with the aid of the intelligent will. He must fix his mind upon the Atman, and never think of anything else. No matter where the restless and the unquiet mind wanders, it must be drawn back and made to submit to the Atman only.

> Utterly quiet,
> Made clean of passion,
> The mind of the yogi
> Knows that Brahman,
> His bliss is the highest.
>
> Released from evil
> His mind is constant
> In contemplation:
> The way is easy,
> Brahman has touched him,
> That bliss is boundless.
>
> His heart is with Brahman,
> His eye in all things
> Sees only Brahman
> Equally present,
> Knows his own Atman
> In every creature,
> And all creation
> Within that Atman.
>
> *— Bhagavad Gita*

Who has no patience, has no strength. Who has no strength, has no contentment. Who has no contentment, has no peace.

— Tradition

$\mathscr{P}$atience —————————————— UNDERSTANDING

Buddhism

Anger is the greatest downfall, and patience, its antidote, is the greatest virtue.

Two Brothers

Once upon a time in India, there was a great king named Brahmadatta who had two sons. Despite all the luxuries of palace life, the older son wished to renounce all worldly attachments and live the spiritual life of a wandering monk. Seeing the steadfast resolve of his beloved son, with great sadness and many tears, the king finally gave his permission. The prince left the comforts of the palace and went to live in solitude in the forest. There he meditated on loving kindness for all beings, befriending and pacifying the wild elephants and lions. Subdued and serene, he became known as Kshativadin, the Patient One.

One day his younger brother, now King Kalabhu, went with his many wives to frolic in the forest. Eventually, he dozed off on a sleepy meadow, and as the women wandered off to pick flowers they came upon the ascetic Kshativadin, meditating peacefully. Attracted by his serene countenance, they bowed before him. When King Kalabhu awoke, he was furious to find his women admiring the sage. Not recognizing his own brother, he drew his sword to attack him. With one blow, he severed both the monk's arms, screaming, "How patient are you now?" When Kshativadin showed no anger, he was further infuriated and cut off both the monk's legs, snarling, "How patient are you now?" Still, Kshativadin remained calm and tranquil, saying, "Although I suffer tremendously, I feel no anger. Instead of cutting off my limbs, you should cut through your own anger and impatience."

As a result of Kalabhu's wicked actions, famine and epidemics raged in the land, creating untold miseries. When the astrologers told Kalabhu that he was to blame, the king went to the forest and bowed before the monk Kshativadin, saying, "I sincerely regret my evil deeds and all the suffering they have caused." To this Kshativadin replied, "Just as a seed produces fruit, so each action we create produces its result. I bear you no grudge, nor do I feel despondent. If this is true, let my body become whole."

With this, his severed limbs became reattached. The king was astonished and, bowing at his feet once more, begged for his mercy and compassion. The sage Kshativadin pledged to free his brother from delusion once he became enlightened, and when he became a Buddha, he did.

A Little Patience Yields Big Results

Once there were two brothers who became monks. The older one was very intelligent, but the younger one, named Chunda, was so stupid that he couldn't remember even one line of the scriptures. He couldn't memorize even the simplest mantra. By the time he got to the end of the line, he had forgotten the beginning. This went on for some years. Chunda tried as hard as he could, but eventually he felt so humiliated and discouraged, he considered giving up the robes.

One day he went to the Buddha and asked why he was so stupid. The Buddha explained that in a past life he had been a learned scholar, but being puffed up with pride, had denigrated the intelligence of others. As a result of this, he was born with low intelligence in this life.

The Buddha hit upon a plan. He asked Chunda to sweep the temple. As he swept, he was asked to repeat the phrase, "Sweep away the dust, sweep away the stains."

Chunda applied himself diligently to the task. With every sweep of the broom, he faithfully recited, "Sweep away the dust, sweep away the stains," day in and day out. With perseverance and continuous practice, gradually he recognized that the dust to be swept away represents karmic obscurations and the stains to be purified are the defilements of the mind. The simple task of sweeping the temple thus became a profound practice. By conscientiously applying himself to this task, Chunda achieved successive stages of realization and eventually liberation.

Catching the Ox

If he tries to detain it,
He does not feel good.
That accounts for the truth
Of their relationship.
To what avail will it be
To get hold of the raging ox?
The harder he pulls on the rein,
The bolder the ox becomes.

Christianity

"Love is patient and kind."   – *Bible, I Corinthians 13:4*

"All the days of my service I would wait, till my release should come."
                                                          – *Bible, Job 14:14*

"Ask, and it will be given you; seek and you will find; knock and it will be opened to you."   – *Bible, Matthew 7:7*

Islam

The Journey

The hoopoe paused, and when the group had heard
His discourse, trembling fear filled every bird.
They saw the bow of this great enterprise
Could not be drawn by weakness, sloth or lies,
And some were so cast down that then and there
They turned aside and perished in despair.
With fear and apprehension in each heart,
The remnant rose up ready to depart.
They travelled [sic] on for years; a lifetime passed
Before the longed-for goal was reached at last.
What happened as they flew I cannot say,
But if you journey on that narrow Way,
Then you will act as they once did and know
The miseries they had to undergo.
Of all the army that set out, how few
Survived the Way; of that great retinue
A handful lived until the voyage was done—
Of every thousand there remained but one.
Of many who set out no trace was found.
Some deep within the ocean's depths were drowned;
Some died on mountaintops; some died of heat;
Some flew too near the sun in their conceit,
Their hearts on fire with love—too late they learned
Their folly when their wings and feathers burned;
Some met their death between the lion's claws,
And some were ripped to death by monsters' jaws;
Some died of thirst; some hunger sent insane,
Till suicide released them from their pain;
Some became weak and could no longer fly
(They faltered, fainted, and were left to die);
Some paused bewildered and then turned aside
To gaze at marvels as if stupefied;
Some looked for pleasure's path and soon confessed
They saw no purpose in the pilgrims' quest;
Not one in every thousand souls arrived—
In every hundred thousand one survived.

[Only those birds that patiently waited (through many difficulties) to achieve their
original goal and did not seek instant gratification completed the journey.]

— *The Conference of the Birds p 213-4*

Ye shall certainly
Be tried and tested
In your possessions
And in your personal selves;
And ye shall certainly
Hear much that will grieve you,
From those who received
The Book before you
And from those who
Worship many gods.
But if ye persevere
Patiently, and guard
Against evil—then
That will be
A determining factor
In all affairs.

— The Meaning of the Holy Qur'an p. 177
3:186

The Prophet was passing by a woman who was weeping near a grave, and he said, 'Fear God, and be patient.' She said, 'Away from me! My calamity has not befallen thee, and thou dost not know it.' The woman was afterwards told that it was the Prophet; whereupon she came to the door of the Prophet where she found no door-keeper. She said to the Prophet, 'I did not know thee, O Prophet of God!' The Prophet said, 'Patience is only (becoming) at the first (stroke) of grief.'

— Selections from Mishkat-ul-masabi [554] p. 123
Anas, BU: MU

Chinese

"Those whose measures are dictated by mere expediency will arouse continual discontent."

— Confucius

"Give me a few more years, so that I may have spent a whole fifty in study, and I believe that after all I should be fairly free from error."

— Confucius

"Clever talk can confound the workings of moral force, just as small impatiences can confound great projects."

– Confucius

The Master said, Even when walking in a party of no more than three I can always be certain of learning from those I am with. There will be good qualities that I can select for imitation and bad ones that will teach me what requires correction in myself.

– The Analects, Book VII

India

Narada and the Two Yogis

The great saint Narada was passing, one day, through a forest. There, in the middle of the forest, he saw a large ant-hill. When ants are digging into the earth to make an underground nest, the soil they carry away is put in a heap nearby. It makes quite a big mound. Narada looked at this ant-hill and was surprised to see that at the top of the ant-hill was a yogi's head.

"What is this?" he thought. "How can there be a yogi's head at the top of an ant-hill?"

He went closer and saw that the yogi's eyes were shut.

"What are you doing here in the middle of an ant-hill?" Narada said in a loud voice.

The yogi opened his eyes and looked at Narada.

"Oh, Narada, it is you!" he said. "How fortunate I am that you have come this way. I came to the forest to meditate, and I have been sitting here meditating for so long that these ants have built their ant-hill round me. Where are you going, Narada?"

"I am on my way to heaven," Narada replied. "I am going to see God."

"Oh, will you see God" the yogi said. "When you see Him, would you ask Him a question for me?"

"Certainly," Narada replied. "What question do you want me to ask Him?"

"What I want to know is," the yogi answered, "how much longer must I sit here meditating? When shall I see God and realize Him so that I do not have to be born again and again? Would you please ask Him that for me?"

"Yes, certainly," Narada assured him, "I will ask God your question." Narada then went on his way through the forest. After some time he began to hear someone singing in a loud voice. Narada walked on, and then he saw the owner of the loud voice. A yogi was jumping about, singing and dancing. As soon as the yogi saw Narada, he ran to him and said, "Narada, Narada, I am so glad to see you. Where are you going?"

"I am going to heaven," Narada replied.

"Oh, are you going to heaven?" cried the yogi. "Then will you do something for me?"

"Yes, certainly," Narada said. "What can I do for you in heaven?"

"Narada," the yogi replied, "I know that I shall have to be born again and again until my heart becomes so pure that I can see God, but what I want to know is, How many times must I be reborn? Please ask God that for me, will you?"

"Yes, certainly," Narada assured him. "I will ask God your question."

Narada walked on and on through the forest, and at last he reached heaven. Narada stayed in heaven for some time, and then went back to earth. He traveled about the earth, visiting many different places, and one day he happened to walk through that same forest, and there he met the yogi who was meditating in the middle of an ant-hill.

"Oh, Narada," said the yogi, "did you ask God about me?"

"Yes," Narada replied, "I did."

"You did? What did He say?" asked the yogi eagerly.

"God told me," Narada said, "that you must go on meditating through four more lives. Then you will be free."

"What? Four more lives?" exclaimed the yogi in despair. "Oh, that is terrible! I have meditated and meditated. I have meditated so long that the ants have built their ant-hill round me! Now you say even that is not enough. I have four more lives! Oh, I am so sad!" And the yogi began to weep.

"You have only four more lives," Narada said quietly. Then he went on his way.

Soon he met the yogi, who was singing and dancing.

"Oh, Narada," said the singing yogi, "did you ask God about me?"

"Yes," replied Narada, "I did."

"You did? What did He say?" asked the singing yogi eagerly.

"Well, now," Narada replied, "you see this tamarind tree? How many leaves has it? Count them. As many leaves as there are on this tamarind tree, so many times you will be born again, and then your heart will become pure and you will see God."

"Oh, how wonderful!" cried the singing yogi. "Narada, your news has made me very happy. I did not think that I would see God so soon. As many leaves as there are on this tamarind tree, that number of times I shall be reborn! Oh, Narada, that is but a short time—and then I shall be free!" Then the yogi began to dance and sing in great joy.

At that moment there was a flash of light, and a voice came from heaven.

"My child," said the voice to the singing yogi, "you are free at this moment. God is pleased with you because you have great patience and strength of mind. The tamarind tree has a great many leaves and yet you are willing to be born again and again as many times as there are leaves on that tree. That shows that you are steadfast and firm in your decision to see God and win your freedom. Therefore, God has made you free here and now. You will not be born again, but you will live with God."

Judaism

The Bird Nest

Once the Baal Shem was in the House of Prayer with his disciples. He was praying for a long time, although his disciples had long since finished. They waited for long while, then they got tired of waiting and went home. He explained to them later that it was a painful separation for him when they left him alone to pray. He told them this parable.

There are birds who fly to warm countries in the autumn. One year the people in one of those warm countries saw a beautiful bird of all colors in the midst of a flock, which was flying on their annual journey. No one had ever seen such a beautiful bird. It perched itself on one of the tallest trees and sat comfortably in its leaves. When the king of this country heard about this bird he commanded some men to make a human ladder which could reach the bird, and get the bird for him. The men stood on each other's shoulders until their formation was high enough to reach the nest. Just before the last man could reach it, the men closest to the ground lost patience and the human ladder collapsed.

PROVERBS AND MAXIMS

Only those who have the patience to do simple things perfectly
will acquire the skill to do difficult things easily. — *Anonymous*

Patience
is a necessary ingredient of genius.
— *Disraeli*

In art one cannot have too much patience.
— *Van Gogh*

**Great works are performed not by strength
but by perseverance.** — *S. Johnson*

**The confidence which we have in ourselves
gives birth to much of that which we have in others.**
— *La Rochefoucauld*

HEROES AND HEROINES

SUSAN B. ANTHONY (1820–1906)

She was born in Adams, Massachusetts, one of seven children; her American ancestry goes back to her family's settlement in Rhode Island in 1634. She attended Quaker schools and began teaching when she was 18. Her family moved to Rochester, New York in 1845, where she was influenced by her father's work with slavery abolitionists like Frederick Douglas. She took up the cause of women's rights in 1851 and began campaigning door to door and with speakers for the rights of women and the abolition of slavery. She organized the National Women's Suffrage Association, was arrested for voting in the 1872 presidential election, and spent the rest of her life working for an amendment to the constitution that would give women the right to vote. She was active until the day she died at age 86. At her death only four states had granted women the right to vote, but the 29th Amendment, enacting this legislation, was passed fourteen years later.

SHIRLEY ANITA ST. HILL CHISHOLM (1924–)

Born in the Bedford-Stuyvesant section of Brooklyn, New York, she was the daughter of emigrant unskilled laborers; her father was from Guyana and her mother was from Barbados. To save money, Shirley was sent to Barbados when she was three years old to live with her grandmother. She recalls being lectured about the virtues of pride, courage, and faith. She returned to Brooklyn at age eleven, graduated from a girl's high school, and entered Brooklyn College to study sociology. She also earned an M.A. degree in elementary education from Columbia University. She became a recognized authority on early education and child welfare, serving as an educational consultant for New York City's bureau of child welfare. At the same time she became involved with the Democratic Women's Workshop, the League of Women Voters, and other local political groups. She entered politics in 1964, becoming the first black woman from Brooklyn to serve in the State Assembly. In 1969 she became the first black woman elected to Congress. Though she seems small and frail in physical stature, her voice on behalf of millions of disinherited Americans has been strong and vital.

MARIE CURIE (1867–1934)

Born in Warsaw, Poland, Marie was a brilliant student, but because Poland did not allow women to attend college, her sister helped her gain entrance to the Sorbonne in Paris in September 1891. In 1894, she began her work with Pierre Curie at the University of Paris. Their friendship resulted in their marriage in 1895 and an extraordinary partnership in scientific work. While searching for sources of radioactivity, they discovered polonium (named after Poland) and radium. Together they published 32 scientific papers, including the announcement that, when exposed to radium, diseased tumor-forming cells were destroyed faster than healthy cells. They jointly received the Nobel Prize in Physics in 1903.

AMELIA MARY EARHART (1897–1937)

Born in Kansas City, Missouri, she lived with her wealthy maternal grandparents in Atheson, Kansas, but spent her summers in Kansas City. Because of her father's struggle with alcoholism, she attended schools in several states and finally ended up in Chicago where the Hyde Park yearbook described her as "A.E.—the girl in brown (her favorite color) who walks alone." After a year at Columbia University, she moved to Los Angeles, where she saw her first air show and took her first airplane ride. She learned to fly but couldn't afford such an expensive hobby so moved back to Boston and became a social worker. In 1928, she joined a crew that was flying across the Atlantic and met her future husband, George Palmer Putnam. He chose her as his "Lady Lindy" (after Charles Lindbergh) and became her manager in arranging flying engagements. She became world famous as the first woman to fly solo across the Atlantic. She became an advocate of aviation and women's rights. On July 2, 1937, she disappeared over the Pacific while trying to circumnavigate the earth.

VIKTOR EMIL FRANKL (1905–1997)

Born in Vienna, Austria and educated at the University of Vienna, he was one of Europe's leading psychiatrists. After three horrible years at Auschwitz and other Nazi prisons, he gained freedom only to learn that almost his entire family had been wiped out. However, during his ordeal and because of his experience in the death camps, he developed his theory of Logotherapy. The suffering and degradations of those harrowing years taught him much about the human spirit, what it takes to become a whole person, and humanity's quest for a higher meaning in life. He became professor of psychiatry and neurology at the University of Vienna and President of the Austrian Medical Society for Psychotherapy. He was a visiting professor at Harvard University and a frequent lecturer around the United States. His experiences in the concentration camp and his theories are found in his book, *Man's Search for Meaning*. His survival and his wisdom are examples of the strength of the human spirit and the power of a belief in God.

MADELEIN L'ENGLE (1918–)

Born in New York City, New York, she was the only child of Charles Wadsworth Camp and Madeline Hall Barnet Camp. Her father was a writer and journalist and her mother was a talented pianist. As a child, Madelein stayed busy reading and writing; she wrote her first book at age five. Because of her father's work she grew up in New York, France, Switzerland and England. She graduated from Smith College in 1941 and pursued graduate studies at the New School for Social Research. She married actor Hugh Franklin in 1946 but continued using the name "Madelein L'Engle" for her writing. She has written poetry, prayers, fantasy, fiction, and novels for adults and young adults; as such, she could easily be thought of as a heroine for creativity, but is included as a model for patience because one of her best known works, *A Wrinkle in Time,* was rejected by more than twenty publishers. She lives in New York with her granddaughter and continues to write.

Patience——————————————EMBRACING

BENJAMIN FRANKLIN (1706–1790)

Born in Boston, Massachusetts, into a family that was religious, frugal and self-reliant, Benjamin was very bright and had a deep desire to learn. Because of economic reasons, he had only two years of formal education, but designed a lifelong career of self-education. He became an apprentice in his brother's printing shops and read everything that passed by. At age fifteen, he began writing social commentaries, but because his brother was tyrannical, often beating him, he ran away to Philadelphia at seventeen. He opened his own print shop and, even though life was difficult, his persistence, patience, and hard work began to pay off. He and a group of friends met every Friday night to discuss current issues and philosophy. Together they founded the first subscription library (1731), a fire company (1736), a public academy for needy boys that eventually became the University of Pennsylvania (1749), and America's first medical center (1751). He became a leading scientist, inventor, publisher, and politician. He was the only founding father to sign all four documents related to America's independence: *The Declaration of Independence, The Treaty with England, The Treaty with France* and *The Constitution.*

BABE DIDRIKSON ZAHARIAS (1914–1956)

Born in Port Arthur, Texas, as Mildred Ella Didrikson, she was one of the greatest American athletes of the first half of the 20th century. She was a record breaker in high school and participated in basketball, baseball, golf, swimming, tennis and volleyball (she wasn't allowed to play football). In college, she was an All-American basketball player. She also won eight events and tied for a ninth in the women's national track and field meet. In the 1932 Olympic games, she earned two gold medals, one for the javelin throw and another for the 80m hurdle event. In 1935 she turned to golf and became the leading U.S. woman golfer, winning 17 straight titles in 1947. She married George Zaharias, a wrestler, in 1938. She developed cancer in 1953 and survived an operation to win two more golf titles in 1954. She is noteworthy not just because she was a gifted athlete, but because of her dedication to excellence, her courageous spirit and her inspiration of women athletes.

PUT PATIENCE INTO ACTION

- Focus on someone or something that ordinarily makes you lose your patience and try to understand it (and don't "lose it").

- Don't give up on difficult jobs or situations.

- When you disagree with someone's strong conviction, keep talking calmly with them; try to understand them.

- Every time there is a situation where someone or something makes you feel impatient take a deep breath and think about it before you do or say anything.

- Extend the limits of your patience every day.

- When faced with a big project, set a series of small goals and accomplish one of them every day.

- Be creative and find something to do or think about when you are waiting for someone.

- Complete an activity which requires patience. Write a story, make a craft, or memorize a poem.

COMMUNITY SERVICE IDEAS

- Help with the paper recycling project at your school.

- Plant a community vegetable garden and give the food to the homeless; get them to help with it. If you can't plant a garden, write letters to managers of food markets asking them to donate food to organizations set up to feed the poor. Follow up on the letters with a visit or phone call.

- Organize a group to take lunch to a Habitat for Humanity work site once a month.

- Volunteer with a local food bank.

- Volunteer with an after-school program to read to younger children or help with playground activities. Be faithful in your attendance.

- Create signs and banners to extol the virtues of patience. Hang them up in public places where you often see people waiting in long lines.

- Volunteer to walk with elderly people to the library, store, church, or park.

- Visit physically handicapped citizens and help around their homes, read to them, play games, fix tea, and listen to stories of their youth.

- Record your grandparents telling their life story, or ask them questions about their childhood and record their answers. Edit your recordings to make them as interesting as possible.

- Share the value of patience at home tonight. Talk about ways to have patience in your family relationships. For example, set a rule that anyone can call a "time out" when a family member has lost his or her patience, or set some other rule unique to your own family's lifestyle.

BOOKS ON PATIENCE

Bringing the Rain to Kapiti Plain. Verna Aardema. New York: Dial Press, 1981.

Grandma Gets Grumpy. Anna G. Hines. Clarion Books/Ticknor & Fields, 1988.

Oxcart Man. Donald Hall. New York: Viking Press, 1979.

Very Busy Spider. Eric Carle. New York: Philomel Books, 1984.

Very Quiet Cricket. Eric Carle. New York: Philomel Books, 1990.

The Book of Virtues. William J. Bennett, ed. New York: Simon and Schuster, 1993.

  "Can't" – p. 567

  "The Crow and the Pitcher" – p. 532

  "Eureka" – p. 562

  "The Gettysburg Address" – p. 568

  "Perseverance" – p. 565

  "The Stars in the Sky" – p. 542

  "The Story of Scarface" – p. 546

  "You Mustn't Quit" – p. 536

Courage

SUPPORTIVE VALUES

Tenacity • Conviction

DEFINITIONS

Firmness of mind and will in danger or difficulty.

Just the sound of the word **courage** makes one think of mental and moral strength. It's a word which challenges us to face and overcome our fears. We sometimes believe that a person of great courage is one who has no fear when in fact they are the ones who have acknowledged and conquered their fear. Cervantes reminds us, "He who loses wealth loses much; he who loses a friend loses more; but he who loses his courage loses all."

Tenacity comes from the Latin root *tenax* which means "tending to hold fast." It is one thing to have courage to think in a moral way but it is quite another to actually follow through on thoughts with actions and to keep following through. It is uncommon to have the tenacity to cling to an idea which may be difficult or dangerous.

Conviction is a strong belief in something. A person with conviction is one who is not easily influenced by his or her peers or environment. A person with conviction is one who does not quit no matter how hard the task. Even in the face of peer pressure or formidable odds, such people are determined to stick to their values and their goals; they have the courage of their convictions.

PURPOSE

In our world of relative abundance, many of the challenges requiring courage which faced our ancestors are no longer a part of our lives. We are sheltered from the elements, and rarely need to face survival situations. The search for physical challenges which test our mettle is all too apparent in the plethora of activities available to us, ranging from endurance contests to thrill-seeking adventures. It seems we are searching for ways to confirm our courage through external experiences, while neglecting the courageous act of looking inward and reflecting on our character. When faced with the pressures of our materialistic culture, we need to summon our courage to discriminate between what we need and what we are influenced to want. Having the courage to understand the inner self is the more difficult task requiring tenacity and mental toughness above and beyond any physical challenge.

February

Courage

Day One: Discuss the meaning of courage using the definitions on page 107.	**Day Two:** Use the discussion questions on page 107 to learn more about courage.	**Day Three:** Brainstorm to make a list of people who must use courage every day at work. (for example, police, firemen, soldiers, and sailors, etc.)
Day Four: Does it take courage to tease a younger student? Why not? What would you say to the student doing the teasing? How would you find the courage to stop the teasing? Role play the situation and its solution.	**Day Five:** Create an award of the week to present to a student who exhibited courage this week. Do this at the end of every week this month.	

Day Six: What types of animals do you think represent bravery? Explain your choices.	**Day Seven:** Does having courage mean you should be reckless? Discuss the differences between courage and recklessness and draw some conclusions about where courage ends and recklessness begins.	**Day Eight:** Choose a bookmark from page 117 that inspires you to have courage. Copy it and put it in a place where you will see it often.
Day Nine: It takes courage to meet new challenges. Have you backed away from any new experiences because you lacked the courage? How can you increase your courage so that you will be ready to take on the next new challenge that comes your way?	**Day Ten:** Some people find courage through friends and family. Remember an experience you had where someone else gave you courage. Draw a picture about your experience.	

Day Eleven: Discuss whether a courageous person can have fear. Don't you think those with true courage are those who fear yet go on? Make up a story about a person who was afraid but continued on a path of courage.	**Day Twelve:** What motivates courage? Remember a time when you were courageous under very difficult circumstances. Where did you get the power to have courage? Share with the class the situation, your actions, and your emotions.	**Day Thirteen:** Read about the courageous acts of the heroes and heroines on pages 118–119. Which act of courage do you most admire? Tell why.
Day Fourteen: Do you think people are born with courage, just as with the color of their eyes, or do they gather courage from experiences in early life? Explain your answers.	**Day Fifteen:** Learn about the life of Helen Keller. Try to imagine how courageous she had to be to continue with her studies in spite of her blindness. Work as partners to take turns blind folding each other and trying to complete some ordinary chores without your sight.	

Day Sixteen: Create a large class banner to celebrate courage. Hang it proudly outside your classroom door.	**Day Seventeen:** Why does it take courage to try something new or to do something in a way you have never done it before? Tell about a time when you really had to convince yourself to try something new, and how it turned out.	**Day Eighteen:** Discuss the kind of courage the first astronauts had to have to be able to blast off into outer space for the first space missions. How do you think their families felt on the day of their launch?
Day Nineteen: Make a "badge of courage" for yourself. Think of something you have done this week which entitles you to wear the badge. If you can't think of anything, do something now. Wear your badge with pride!	**Day Twenty:** Reflect on what you have learned this month about courage. Do you feel you are ready to accept courage as a lifelong value? If so, how can you begin to practice courage in daily life? If not, what can you do to become more courageous?	

COURAGE IN OTHER LANGUAGES

Chinese	*yong*	brave; daring courage
French	*le courage*	strength of character, steadiness or resoluteness in the face of danger, suffering or difficult situations; zeal for undertaking something or a strong desire to do something
German	*beherzt*	brave, spirited, stouthearted, courageous
Hawaiian	*wiwo'ole*	fearless, brave, bold ('wiwo' means "fearful, bashful, modest, afraid, timid, shy" and 'ole' means "not, without, lacking"—literally, wiwo'ole means "no fear")
Japanese	*yuuki*	gush out spiritual energy
Korean	*yong ki*	brave spirit
Latin	*virtus*	from Latin "cor" (heart) (action in accordance with one's heart)
Spanish	*coraje*	courage, bravery, valor
Tagalog	*katapangan*	fearless bravery in the face of physical, moral or spiritual danger

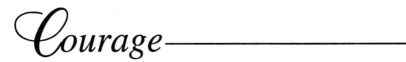

DISCUSSION QUESTIONS

• Have you been faced with a decision that required courage?

• What resources do you draw from in making difficult decisions?

• What makes a person right—age, wealth, power, fame, or virtue? Why?

• Give an example of something you have a strong opinion about. What could make you change your mind? How do you know when you should?

• Were you afraid of something as a young child that no longer scares you? How did you overcome this fear?

• Can the same principle be applied to all fears?

• Have you ever been pressured into doing something you later regretted or realized was wrong? Do you have the courage to decide differently today?

• Where does conviction come from? What is something for which you have a strong conviction?

STORIES AND THOUGHTS FROM SPIRITUAL TRADITIONS

Buddhism

The greatest courage is not in conquering enemies outside, but conquering the enemies of hatred, attachment, and ignorance within one's own mind.

Zen Buddhism

When there is fullness, success is certain; where there is hollowness, uncertain.

Christianity

"Do not be overcome by evil, but overcome evil with good."
– Bible, Romans 12:21

"Be strong, and let your heart take courage."
– Bible, Psalm 31:24

"As you know, we had courage in our God in the face of great opposition."
– Bible, I Thessalonians 2:2

Islam

The bravest is the most in control of himself.

The Prophet asked his companions: "Whom do you consider brave?"
"One who triumphs in a wrestling match," suggested some of the companions.
"Not so," the Prophet corrected them. "It is rather one who controls himself when he is angry."
– God-oriented Life p. 82

Chinese

"He who rules by moral force is like the pole-star, which remains in its place while the lesser stars do homage to it."
– Confucius

"Just as to sacrifice to ancestors other than one's own in presumption, so to see what is right and not do it is cowardice."

– Confucius

"A Good Man will certainly also possess courage; but a brave man is not necessarily Good."

– Confucius

Tzu-lu said, "Is courage to be prized by a gentleman?" The Master said, "A gentleman gives the first place to Right. If a gentleman has courage but neglects Right, he becomes turbulent. If a small man has courage but neglects Right, he becomes a thief."

– The Analects, Book XVII

American

Wiley and the Hairy Man

Down by the edge of a swamp, in a small cabin, there lived a boy named Wiley and his mama. Now strange things were known to happen every now and then in those parts. For instance, dogs would start barking wildly for no reason, strange figures would be spotted running through the woods, and laughter could be heard from time to time amongst the trees. People said it might be the Hairy Man up to some mischief.

Each time Wiley would set out from the house his mama would call, "You be careful now, Wiley. You look out for that Hairy Man, y'hear? Never know when he'll be up to no good."

Wiley would reply cheerfully, "Don't you worry, Mama. Got my hound dogs with me all the time, everywhere I go. You know that Hairy Man just can't stand hound dogs!"

Wiley's mama would smile, for indeed she knew that the Hairy Man couldn't abide those hound dogs. In fact, Wiley's mama knew all sorts of things, including a little bit of conjure magic!

One day, Wiley set out to gather a load of wood nearby, so he left his faithful dogs tied up on the porch. Before he knew it he had wandered deep into the swamp in search of wood. He was a lot farther away from home than he had expected to be when he felt a shiver go down his spine. He heard some branches cracking and he spun around quick to see the Hairy Man coming his way.

Oh, was he an ugly fellow! Big and hairy all over with a slobbery yellow grin. It was a crazy grin, and Wiley was not pleased at all to be meeting him. The Hairy Man galloped wildly toward Wiley and stopped suddenly, a couple of inches from his face. "Hello, Wiley," said the Hairy Man in a husky sort of voice.

"Don't you come so close to me, Mister Hairy Man," insisted Wiley. He looked down at the Hairy Man's strange feet only to discover that they weren't feet at all. They were hooves! Now Wiley knew that those weren't feet for climbing, so he scrambled up the nearest tree as fast as he could.

"You come on down, Wiley!" hollered the Hairy Man.

"No sir, Mister Hairy Man. Come on up 'n get me if you want," replied Wiley.

The Hairy Man kept smiling his awful smile. "I'll just be down here waiting for you, Wiley. I'll be waiting until nightfall. Just until you get hungry or tired," the Hairy Man chuckled.

Now Wiley wasn't going to give up to this ugly old Hairy Man. He remembered his dogs back home on the porch and he came up with a plan. "Say, Mister Hairy Man, I hear tell you know some conjure magic," said Wiley.

"Why, I know more conjure magic than anyone in these parts!" boasted the Hairy Man.

"Well," said Wiley, "I'll bet you don't know enough to make something disappear. How 'bout making that tree stump disappear? Can you do that?"

In an instant the tree stump disappeared. "Now, you see that, Wiley? It's gone!"

"Is that all the conjure magic you have, Mister Hairy Man? Let's see you make my shirt disappear," Wiley called down.

"Gone!" cried the Hairy Man as Wiley's shirt vanished.

"You're going to run out of conjure magic soon, Mister Hairy Man. Bet you can't even make this little rope holding up my britches disappear."

"Sure, I can!" yelled the Hairy Man. "Why I can make every rope in this county disappear now!"

Wiley began to chuckle as he held onto his britches. "Oh yes, you know some mighty wonderful conjure magic. Just the magic I needed, in fact. Here dogs! Here dogs!" Wiley called to his dogs that the Hairy Man had just freed from the porch by magic.

Wiley could hear his dogs barking as they ran toward the swamp from the house. The Hairy Man did not wait for the dogs to get any closer, he just turned and ran faster than lightning away into the swamp.

When Wiley and his dogs made it home, Wiley told his mama how he had fooled the Hairy Man. His mama gave him a big hug and said, "Well now, you've fooled the Hairy Man once, son. If you can manage to outwit him two more times he'll stay away for good!"

"I hope I don't have occasion to run into him ever again," said Wiley. "Can't say I like the looks of that hairy face, or that slobbery grin, or those big black hooves."

"Say, Wiley," asked his mama, "did you happen to see if he was carrying a sack?"

"'Matter of fact he was, Mama," nodded Wiley.

"Well, I just thought of another way you can fool that Hairy Man, Wiley," said his mama. "Now listen, you go on into the swamp tomorrow without the dogs and here's what you do." Wiley's mama gave him a plan to trick the Hairy Man once more.

The next morning, Wiley left his faithful dogs shut inside the cabin and walked off toward the swamp. He tried whistling and singing and hopping on one foot to keep his courage up and his mind off the Hairy Man. Then all at once, he felt that same shiver up his spine from the day before.

Suddenly, standing right before him was the Hairy Man.

"Hello again, Wiley," said the Hairy Man, grinning his wicked grin.

"Well, hello there, Mister Hairy Man," said Wiley, trying to smile. "What have you got in that big old sack there?"

"Nothing, Wiley. At least, not yet!" said the Hairy Man, leaning real close to Wiley and laying his sack down right next to him.

"Say, Mister Hairy Man," said Wiley, looking him straight in the eye, "I hear tales of how you can change yourself into any old animal you want. Could they be true?"

"Yes, Wiley," said the Hairy Man, bending right over him, "those tales are true." Now the Hairy Man looked mighty fierce, but Wiley went on.

"You wouldn't be able to change yourself into something big like a bear, would you?" asked Wiley. Before he knew it the Hairy Man had disappeared

and there in his place was a huge black bear, grinning and slobbering at Wiley. "I'm impressed," said Wiley, trying to sound brave. "But I bet you can't turn yourself into, say, an alligator."

In an instant the bear vanished and Wiley was looking at the mouth of an alligator, smiling and slobbering at him. "Oh, I see you're mighty fine at turning yourself into something big," said Wiley, "but I bet you can't change into something small, like, for instance, a possum."

Just as Wiley had hoped, the alligator was gone in a flash and in its place was a tiny possum. Wiley scooped up the little animal and shoved it into the sack which lay on the ground. He tied it up real tight and sent it flying into the river. Then he turned and started back home. He was feeling pretty good about outwitting the Hairy Man for the second time when he heard a deep voice bellowing from the river.

"I'm going to get you, Wiley! You just wait and see!" the Hairy Man's voice boomed through the swamp.

With that, Wiley ran as fast as his legs could go. When he arrived back at the cabin huffing and puffing he told his mama what had happened.

"Well now, son," Wiley's mama said as she patted him on the back, "you've managed to trick that Hairy Man twice. I imagine he's good and angry now. We'll just have to come up with a way to fool him again and we'll be rid of him forever and always."

Now Wiley did not like the idea of the Hairy Man coming to his house to get him, but Wiley's mama was calm as she rocked in her rocking chair and came up with a plan. "Wiley," she said, "go to the barn and bring back one of our baby pigs." Wiley did as he was told, but on his way to the barn he thought he saw a strange, wild animal run through the trees. It was as large as a horse, but it had curly hair. His dogs ran barking after it and they disappeared into the trees.

Wiley brought the little pig into the cabin. "Now go and put that baby pig in your bed, Wiley," said his mama, "and pull the covers up over it nice and tight." Just as he was covering up the piglet he got that peculiar shiver up his spine and he could hear thumping and scraping all around the cabin walls. The whole cabin began to shake and Wiley began to tremble a bit, as well.

Suddenly there was a great banging on the door. "Quick, Wiley," his mama whispered, "climb up into the loft and stay out of sight!" Then, quite calmly, Wiley's mama opened the door.

"Where's your boy?" the Hairy Man yelled. "I've come to get him!"

"Well, you can't have him," said Wiley's mama.

"Then I'll have to bite you," said the Hairy Man, stepping closer.

"Well, I suppose I'll have to bite you right back," said Wiley's mama, looking him square in the eye.

"Give him to me, or I'll set your house afire!" threatened the Hairy Man.

"Oh, I've plenty of milk to put out your fire," said Wiley's mama.

"I say give him to me, or I'll make your cow run away, I'll make your well go dry, and I'll make your cotton shrivel and die," yelled the Hairy Man.

"Oh, you wouldn't do all those awful things, would you, Mister Hairy Man? You couldn't be that horrible, could you?" Wiley's mama said in her sweetest voice.

"I can be that horrible and I will!" screamed the Hairy Man.

"Oh, well," said Wiley's mama, "I suppose I should give you my baby then." She turned toward Wiley's bed, then turned back toward the Hairy Man. "If I give him to you, do you swear you'll do me no harm and never come back?"

"I do swear, just give him to me!" the Hairy Man bellowed.

"Go on and take him then," said Wiley's mama, pointing to the bed.

The Hairy Man charged over to the bed and threw off the covers. "There's nothing but a baby pig here!" he yelled.

"Did I say what kind of baby I was giving you? He's mine and I'm giving him to you. Go on, Mister Hairy Man, take him, he belongs to you now." Wiley's mama smiled sweetly at the Hairy Man. "And remember, Mister Hairy Man, you swore you'd leave me be and never come back if I gave you my baby!"

The Hairy Man went wild as he had been fooled for the third time. He stomped about and gnashed his slobbery teeth, then he tore out of the cabin never to be seen in those parts again.

Wiley climbed down from the loft and ran into his mama's arms. Then he called to his dogs who ran in happily from the woods. "We did it, didn't we, Mama? We tricked that awful old Hairy Man three times over!"

"We did, Wiley," smiled Wiley's mama. "Just you and me against that big old Hairy Man."

PROVERBS AND MAXIMS

Courage is resistance to fear, mastery of fear—not absence of fear.

– *M. Twain*

One man with courage makes a majority.

– *A. Jackson*

Moral courage is a rarer commodity than bravery in battle or great intelligence. Yet it is the one essential, vital quality for those who seek to change a world that yields most painfully to change.   – *R. Kennedy*

It takes courage for a man to listen to his own goodness and act on it. Do we dare be ourselves? This is the question that counts.   – *P. Casals*

We need people who influence their peers and who cannot be detoured from their convictions by peers who do not have the courage to have any convictions.

– *J. Paterno*

HEROES AND HEROINES

DAW AUNG SAN SUU KYI (1945–)

Born in Rangoon, Burma, she is the daughter of General Aung San Kyi, who was the national leader of Burma until he was assassinated in 1947. She studied politics at Delhi University, while her mother served as ambassador to India and Nepal in 1960. She graduated in 1967 from St. Hugh's College, Oxford University with a degree in philosophy, politics, and economics. In 1988, she returned to Burma to help with her ailing mother, and witnessed the student protests in Rangoon. Drawn into the struggle, she proposed the formation of a People's Consultative Committee during the democratic uprising and on August 26, 1988 addressed a mass rally of 500,000 people, calling for a democratic government. The National League for Democracy was formed and Aung San Suu Kyi was elected secretary general. In the next months she gave hundreds of addresses across Burma, narrowly escaped assassination, and was finally put under house arrest, where she stayed until July 10, 1995. Her non-violent struggle and writing earned her the Nobel Peace Prize in 1991.

ANNE FRANK (1929–1945)

Born in Frankfurt, Germany, she enjoyed a good home with her parents and her sister Margot. After the Nazis took over Germany in 1933, the family moved to Amsterdam, Holland. Anne attended the Montessori School, but when the Nazis occupied Holland in 1940 she was forced to leave the school. When Margot received orders for deportation, Mr. Frank was prepared and moved his family, a second family of three, and an eighth man into two small apartments hidden in the rear of the warehouse where he worked. Friends supplied them with necessities, and they remained quiet during working hours and hidden during the night. They were betrayed, arrested, and sent to Auschwitz, a concentration camp. Later they were sent to Bergen Belsen, where Anne perished. Her personal diary became famous as an example of courage and faith and as an account of life under the Nazi terror.

PROM GOULD (1979–)

Prom was born in Cambodia about the time a Vietnamese invasion ended the genocide of the Khmer Rouge regimes of Pol Pot, responsible for the massacre of 4 million people. He was orphaned by the civil war that followed. When his adoptive parents, Ron and Kim Gould of Honolulu, met Prom, he was twelve years old, weighed 40 pounds and suffered from hemophilia, hepatitis, parasites, malaria, and malnutrition. The Goulds were in Cambodia to complete the adoption procedures for their son Mina and noticed Prom taking care of the younger children. Clearly in a lot of pain, he still had a zest for life, showed an interest in everything around him, and exhibited a courage far beyond his years. When the Goulds learned that adoption procedures between Prom and his projected family had failed, they were given the opportunity of adopting him. They didn't hesitate, and Prom was welcomed into their family. With love, medical care, and a lot of food, Prom thrived. His courageous spirit has taken on many challenges: learning English, adapting to a new culture, gaining entrance to school, and learning to paddle outriggers are just a few of his accomplishments. There are more challenges ahead and Prom will meet them with the same optimism, cheerfulness, confidence, and inner strength that delivered him from the horrors of Cambodia.

HELEN KELLER (1880–1968)

Born in Tuscumbia, Alabama, she was deprived of sight and hearing at the age of 19 months due to a severe illness, and soon became mute. She lived in silence and darkness for five years until her parents appealed to Alexander Graham Bell for advice about her education. Ann Sullivan, who was then twenty years old and partially cured of blindness, began to instruct Helen on March 2, 1887. With Ann Sullivan's discipline and dedication, Helen learned the gift of language in one month, learned to read braille, learned to talk, and in 1904 graduated from Radcliffe College. Her education and training represent one of the most extraordinary accomplishments ever achieved in the education of those with similar disabilities. She worked until her death at the age of 88 to help others by writing articles and books, by speaking, and by raising two million dollars for the American Foundation for the Blind. Her greatest gift was the inspiration of her determination and courage.

ROSA LEE MCCAULEY PARKS (1913–)

The early life of this young girl, born in Tuskegee, Alabama, gave no indication that she was destined for greatness. Her mother was a teacher and her father was a carpenter. The family moved to Pine Level, Alabama while Rosa was still young, and she was shielded from the harsh realities of racial segregation. She attended high school and college for a short time in Montgomery. She married Raymond Parks in 1932; they were both active in the voter registration aspect of the civil rights movement. She worked for the NAACP to break down the barriers of segregation in education and public accommodations; little progress was made in the 1940s and early 1950s. In 1955, while working in a Montgomery department store as a tailor's assistant, she made national headlines when she simply refused to give up her seat to a white passenger on a racially segregated bus. Her arrest led to a successful boycott of the Montgomery buses by African-American riders. She is still active in civil rights issues.

JACKIE ROBINSON (1919–1972)

Born in Cairo, Georgia as John Roosevelt Robinson, he was the youngest of five children. His sharecropper father abandoned his family five months after Jackie was born, and his mother, determined to create a better life for her family, moved them all to Pasadena, California when Jackie was only sixteen months old. As Jackie grew up he developed into a sensational athlete and was the first person to earn letters in football, basketball, baseball and track at UCLA. In 1941, after college, he played football with the Los Angeles Bulldogs; however, World War II ended his football career. He began playing baseball in 1945 with the Monarchs of the Negro American Baseball league. Branch Rickey of the Brooklyn Dodgers became aware of his abilities and, with his own act of courage, invited Jackie in 1947 to break the color barrier that existed in major league baseball. In spite of the pressure and prejudice, he played well and was voted Rookie of the Year. It was his spectacular play that led to the Dodgers' first World Series Championship in 1955. His courage was displayed not only on the baseball diamond but also in public, where he spoke out against prejudice and injustice. He retired from baseball in 1956. In later life he suffered quietly and courageously from diabetes, and died from diabetic complications at age 53.

PUT COURAGE INTO ACTION

- Politely disagree with friends when you think they are wrong.

- Develop a strong character by practicing all of the values of the month.

- Choose friends who share these virtues of strong character.

- Make a list of the things about which you have a strong conviction.

- "Stand up" for what you believe (have the courage of your convictions).

- Write your legislator about a cause you believe in.

- Try something different, perhaps a hobby, sport, or activity you've been interested in but afraid to try.

- Have regular conversations with your peers and with adult friends about your personal convictions.

COMMUNITY SERVICE IDEAS

- Write a letter to the editor of your local newspaper about a local injustice.

- Volunteer for an agency that is working to save endangered species.

- Volunteer for a political candidate who has social justice issues and environmental concerns as part of his/her platform.

- Volunteer at the Institute for Human Services to serve food to the homeless.

- Find a community organization serving troubled teenagers and volunteer to serve as a peer listener or to work in other ways within the program.

BOOKS ON COURAGE

All the Lights in the Night. Arthur A. Levine. New York: Tambourine Books, 1991.

Amazing Grace. Mary Hoffman. New York: Dial Books for Young Readers, 1991.

Call it Courage. Armstrong Sperry. New York: MacMillan Company, 1970.

Follow the Drinking Gourd. Bernadine Connelly. Lincoln: GPN, 1993.

The Girl Who Loved Caterpillars. Jean Merrill. New York: Philomel Books, 1992.

John Henry. Julius Lester. New York: Dial Books, 1994.

Little Engine that Could. Waty Piper. New York: Platt & Monk, 1930.

Loop the Loop. Barbara Dugan. New York: Greenwillow, 1992.

Sir Cedric. Roy Gerard. New York: Farrar, Straus & Giroux, 1984.

Teammates. Peter Galenboch. San Diego: Harcourt Brace, Jovanovich, 1990.

The Book of Virtues. William J. Bennett, ed. New York: Simon and Schuster, 1993.

    "The Brave Three Hundred" – p. 472

    "Crossing the Rubicon" – p. 477

    "I Have A Dream" – p. 572

    "If " – p. 476

    "The Minotaur" – p. 463

    "Our Heroes" – p. 461

    "The Road Not Taken" – p. 523

    "Rosa Parks" – p. 489

    "Ulysses and the Cyclops" – p. 467

Creativity

SUPPORTIVE VALUES

Wonder • Resourcefulness

DEFINITIONS

The ability to bring into existence, to produce through imagination.

Creativity is the ability to bring into existence or to form through imaginative skill. These definitions speak to us of the ability to invent. They describe everything from the visual and performing arts to engineering and the theoretical sciences. It is this ability to be thoughtful and imaginative in our work (which makes us creators in the world) that we want to celebrate this month.

Wonder is an excitedly amazed admiration or astonishment at something awesomely mysterious or new to one's experience.

Resourcefulness is the capability of devising ways and means to handle a situation. The ability to creatively use our resources as individuals, as communities, and as a world are at the crux of this value.

PURPOSE

The ability to create is the distinguishing characteristic of being human. Creativity can be a difficult undertaking because the process is personal; sharing a part of yourself. Recognizing the vulnerability of creativity, Beethoven wrote: "Advise your critics to exercise more care and good sense with regard to the productions of young authors; for many a one of them may lose their creative spirit, who otherwise might have risen to higher things."

Educators need to nurture the fragile seedling of creativity in students, urging it to take root, grow strong, blossom, and bear fruit. Many students have been told exactly what to do so often that they are stumped when given an assignment which they can present as they choose. Educators need to take more care with pruning methods and be generous with the fertilizer of encouragement to insure growth. In this way students will discover fulfillment in the creative process and continue to seek and realize their own areas of creativity.

Sustaining a sense of wonder and resourcefulness as educators and nurturing these senses in students are the responsibilities of an educator, for it is wonder which inspires our powers of creativity.

Creativity

Day One:
Use the definitions on page 123 as a springboard for a total class discussion on the meaning of creativity.

Day Two:
Creativity has been defined as "doing something in a new and different way from the way you have ever done it or seen it done before." Agree or disagree with this definition and explain your answer.

Day Three:
Write your very own definition of creativity and tell how that definition applies to and influences your life today. Compare and discuss definitions with a partner.

Day Four:
Using your own definition of creativity and a rating scale of one through four, rate your own creativity.
1) not very creative
2) somewhat creative
3) more creative than the average person of my age
4) extremely creative

Day Five:
Use your creativity to write a haiku.

Day Six:
As a class, use your creativity to think of a way to creatively display your haiku.

Day Seven:
Read the list of words in other languages on page 125. Imagine the creativity it takes to develop a unique language! With a partner, create your own language! Create a list of twenty words complete with definitions (for example, miak = hello).

Day Eight:
Using your new list of vocabulary words, write a paragraph. It won't be easy, but it will give you a great opportunity to challenge your creative abilities!

Day Nine:
Exchange your word lists and paragraph with another group. Decipher the paragraph using the mini-dictionary you were given.

Day Ten:
Many of life's problems can be solved if you are resourceful. Remember a time when your creative abilities helped you solve a problem. Write about it in a journal entry.

Day Eleven:
Organize a school spirit assembly where each class may perform an original song for the entire school!

Day Twelve:
Read a story about creation from the selection on pages 127–132.

Day Thirteen:
Remembering the creation story you heard yesterday, use your imagination to write your own creation story!

Day Fourteen:
Choose a community service project on page 136 to share the gift of creativity.

Day Fifteen:
Put your community service project into action!

Day Sixteen:
Choose a proverb bookmark from the list on page 133. Color it, cut it out, and use it every day!

Day Seventeen:
Creativity can mean lots of fun. In small groups, think of a new game. Be sure to write down all the rules, so that everyone can easily understand how to play. Try to keep it simple and make it a game that everyone can play.

Day Eighteen:
Play the games. Evaluate the creativity of each.

Day Nineteen:
Read about the heroes and heroines who embraced creativity on pages 134–135. Which one would you most like to emulate? Tell why.

Day Twenty:
Reflect on the lessons of creativity you have learned this month and begin now to enrich your life by embracing creativity as an important lifelong value.

CREATIVITY IN OTHER LANGUAGES

Chinese	*chuang*	to create, to make, to invent, to begin
	zao	to create, to make, to build, to prepare, to begin from
French	*la créativité*	ability to use one's imagination and inventive powers to create, for example, literary or artistic works
German	*schöpferisch*	from schöpfer: to scoop, to be generative, productive, creative
Hawaiian	*makaku*	creative imagination of an artist (maka means "eye" but also means "beginning, commencement, source" and one of many definitions of forku is "to appear, show, reveal . . . to change into, transform")
Japanese	*soozoo*	to create something from wood with a knife (soo—"to cut with a knife, to make something for a first time"; zoo—"to carve with an axe")
Latin	*cogitatio*	from Latin "creare" (to make) (the ability to make things)
Spanish	*facultad creadora*	ability to be creative, original
Tagalog	*pagkamalikhain*	pagka—the essence of something, its nature; likhain—to make something never made before

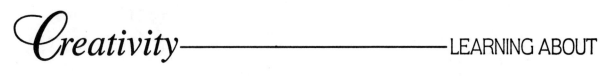
DISCUSSION QUESTIONS

- Who are some creative people you admire? Why are they good models?

- How do you get in touch with your own creativity?

- How would you define a sense of wonder?

- How does being resourceful help solve problems?

- What is the source of human creativity? How can we tap that source?

- What has been your most creative moment?

- What is something in life about which you have a deep feeling of awe and wonder? How can this be inspiring?

- What are the obstacles to solving difficult personal and community problems?

- How creative are you? Are there ways to increase your creativity?

- Are some people more creative than others? Or are there just different kinds of creativity?

STORIES AND THOUGHTS FROM SPIRITUAL TRADITIONS

Hinduism

The world existed first as seed, which as it grew and developed took on names and forms. As a razor in its case or as fire in wood, so dwells the Self, the Lord of the universe, in all forms, even to the tips of the fingers. Yet the ignorant do not know him, for behind the names and forms he remains hidden. When one breathes, one knows him as breath; when one speaks, one knows him as speech; when one sees, one knows him as the eye; when one hears, one knows him as the ear; when one thinks, one knows him as the mind. All these are but names related to his acts; and he who worships the Self as one or another of them does not know him, for of them he is neither one nor another. Wherefore let a man worship him as the Self, and as the Self alone. The perfection, which is the Self, is the goal of all beings. For by knowing the Self one knows all. He who knows the Self is honored of all men and attains to blessedness.

– Upanishads

Buddhism

The greatest creativity is transforming our own mind from ignorance to wisdom, awaking all our inner qualities.

All that we see and hear and feel is a product of the mind. We can create a violent, miserable existence or a loving, happy existence. We are the producer and director of our own movie. We can be miserable or we can be happy. The choice is up to us.

In Tibetan Buddhism there is a practice of imagining oneself as an enlightened being, in an enlightened form with enlightened speech and an enlightened mind. As one teacher in America put it, "If you're not enlightened, pretend you're enlightened!" Through creative imaging, we can embody all enlightened qualities.

Another practice is to imagine our enemy as our greatest teacher. When someone insults or irritates us, instead of retaliating in a similar way, we imagine the person as our dear parent, teacher, or friend, surrounded by love in the form of pure light. This practice has the power to dispel the anger and resentment in our mind, and calm the attacker, too!

Respect the changes which inspiration makes in oneself, without analyzing them or calculating (their results). Success will always come when the heart is without disturbance.

Christianity

"Create in me a clean heart, O God, and put a new and right spirit within me."
– Bible, Psalm 51:10

"You are the light of the world. Let your light so shine before others, that they may see your good works."
– Bible, Matthew 5:14,16

Islam

An Arabic-speaking poet once came into the presence of a king. Now the king was a Turk, and did not know even Persian. The poet had composed in the king's honour some brilliant verses in Arabic and had brought these with him. When the king had taken his seat on the throne and the courtiers were all present and duly stationed, commanders and ministers each in his place, the poet rose to his feet and began to recite his poem. At every passage meriting applause the king nodded his head, while at every passage provoking astonishment he looked amazed; similarly he took note of every passage expressing submission. The courtiers were astounded.

'Our king did not know a word of Arabic,' they murmured amongst themselves. 'How is it that he nodded his head so appositely? He must have known Arabic all these years and kept it secret from us. If we have ever uttered any incivilities in Arabic, then woe betide us!'

Now the king had a favourite slave. The courtiers therefore assembled together and gave him a horse and a mule and a sum of money, and engaged to present him with as much again.

'Just inform us whether or not the king knows Arabic,' they said to him. 'If he does not, how was it that he nodded just at the right places? Was it a miracle? Was it divine inspiration?'

Finally, one day the slave found his opportunity. The king was out hunting, and he perceived that he was in a good humour because much game had been taken. He therefore asked the king point blank. The king burst out laughing.

'By Allah, I don't know Arabic,' he said. 'As for my nodding and applauding, I knew of course what his object was in composing that poem and so I nodded and applauded.'

So it was realised that the root of the matter was the object in view; the poem itself was merely the branch of that object. If it had not been for the object, the man would never have composed that poem.

– Discourses of Rumi p. 346

Chinese

"A craftsman, if he means to do good work, must first sharpen his tools."
– Confucius

"Despise thy masterpieces; thus renew the vigor of your creation. Let the straight appear crooked to you, your craft clumsiness; your Music discord."
– Lao Tzu

American

Apellamando's Dreams

Once upon a time, there was a simple little road which led to a drab little village, which was filled with dull little buildings and surrounded by gray little houses. The streets were quiet, folks worked hard, and the children minded their parents.

Now, just outside this village, there lived a very special boy named Apellamando. What made him so special was that whenever he dreamed dreams or thought thoughts, his dreams and thoughts would appear in brilliant colors above his head. They would float into the air in bright beautiful pictures. If Apellamando thought about a rainbow, a rainbow would sail up from his forehead. If he thought about a butterfly, a lovely butterfly would hang lightly over his head.

Apellamando managed to keep his gift a secret, except from his four best friends. His friends loved to watch Apellamando's dream float against the sky. "Dream of sailboats, Apellamando!" they would cry. "Think of green and yellow caterpillars, Apellamando!" they would beg. Apellamando was happy to grant his friends wishes and they would lie on a patch of grass, and watch Apellamando's colorful dreams in all their glorious colors decorate the sky.

One day, as the friends enjoyed watching bright yellow canaries, bunches of balloons, orange and black tigers, and bouquets of flowers drift from Apellamando's head, it began to rain. As the rain fell, it seemed to moisten Apellamando's floating visions and they began to stick to things!

The bright yellow canaries floated over and stuck fast to the door of the bakery. The bunch of balloons stuck to the walls of the Village Square. There were all of Apellamando's colorful dreams stuck to the walls of the gray little houses and the drab little buildings! The children stood stunned in the street when the baker stepped out of his shop and cried, "Who painted these birds on my door?" He spotted the children and yelled, "What do you think you're doing painting all over our clean little village?"

"I'm sorry. I didn't mean for the dreams to stick. But they do add something quite lovely to the gray walls, don't you think?" said an apologetic Apellamando.

"No, I don't think!" yelled the baker in reply. "In fact I think you children should be punished for painting on our property!"

"But you don't understand," the children cried in unison. By this time, many of the townspeople emerged from the buildings. "How dare the children do this to our walls! They must explain themselves!"

When the children tried to explain themselves, the grown-ups became angrier. "No one can make pictures in his head for all to see. No one can share their colorful dreams," the grown-ups said. They decided the children must be lying. The children were sent home to wait for their punishment.

Apellamando hung his head as they left the village streets and headed for the path through the woods to their homes. His friends tried to reassure him, saying it wasn't his fault. Anyway, they liked the buildings so much better with Apellamando's dreams on them. But Apellamando could not be comforted. "I shall never have another dream. Not ever," he sighed.

"But Apellamando, you can't stop dreaming! We love your dreams!" his friends implored.

"No. Never again," Apellamando insisted.

The children walked forlornly through the woods as the sun began to set. They were too unhappy to mind where they were going, and it began to grow dark before they had reached their homes. Finally, they realized that night was about to fall and they were lost.

Hungry, tired, and a bit worried, the children sat down in a clearing.

"This is all my fault," said Apellamando sadly. "I should never have dreamed those dreams."

"But your dreams are lovely," said one friend.

"Yes, and so colorful," said another.

"We loved to look at them. They made us happy," they all agreed.

"But they were good for nothing," Apellamando said dejectedly.

"Wait a minute," said one of the children, "they would be really good for something now, Apellamando."

"No. My mind's made up. I'll not dream another dream ever," Apellamando replied.

"But Apellamando, if you could dream a dream now, it would float up into the air and the grown-ups would see us and find us."

"Yes, please, Apellamando!" the other chimed in.

"I can't!" said Apellamando.

"You must!" cried his friends.

So, reluctantly, Apellamando began thinking of rainbows and sparrows and apple trees, and slowly his dreams floated higher and higher until they hung in the violet sky.

The children's parents had begun to worry, as their children had not arrived home. They had gathered folks from the village to help look for them. All at once, someone yelled, "Look!" and pointed to the beautiful images floating over the woods.

In a short while the village folk found the children and realized they had been wrong about Apellamando. He really could share his colorful dreams. And what a gift it was!

The village is no longer drab and gray. Its walls are splashed with color and its people are happy. There is an old man that the children visit in the Village Square each day. He tells them wonderful stories, and every now and then a beautiful, colorful picture floats up and rests just above his head for everyone to see.

PROVERBS AND MAXIMS

Happiness lies in the joy of achievement and the thrill of creative effort.

— *F. D. Roosevelt*

The soul should always stand ajar,
ready to welcome the ecstatic experience.

— *Dickinson*

He who can no longer pause to wonder and stand rapt in awe,
is as good as dead; his eyes are closed.

— *Einstein*

My heart leaps up when I behold a rainbow in the sky.
So it was when I was a child, so let it be when I grow old
or let me die.

— *Wordsworth*

Wonder is very much the affection of a philosopher;
for there is no other beginning of philosophy than this.

— *Plato*

HEROES AND HEROINES

LEONARDO DA VINCI (1452–1519)

Born in Vinci, Italy, Leonardo was raised by his father. He became an apprentice of Andrea del Verrochio, a sculptor, painter and goldsmith. For about twenty years, age thirty to fifty, he worked in various capacities as an engineer and architect of cathedrals, a decorator of palaces, an organizer of pageants, and a painter and sculptor, while teaching himself Latin and carrying out anatomical and other scientific research. He served as a painter for a variety of patrons in Milan, Rome, and several French cities. Though there is a scarcity of his paintings, some are well known: *Adoration of the Magi*, *The Last Supper*, and *Mona Lisa*. There is even less of his sculpturing. However, the drawings and sketches of his notebooks show a mixture of social commentary, an interest in ugliness and beauty, a skill in mechanical and anatomical drawing, scientific insight into flying machines, stink bombs, and all kinds of fascinating contraptions, and observations related to geology, geography, botany and astronomy.

CHARLES JOHN HUFFAM DICKENS (1812–1870)

Born in Landport, England (later Portsmouth), he spent his early years on the southern coast, where his father worked for the Navy Pay Office. After losing his job, his father moved the family to London, but things didn't improve. A creditor forced his family into a debtors' prison where they stayed for three months. At age 12, Charles worked in a blacking factory and attended school, where punishment was delivered by blows to his back with a swordlike cane. He worked for a time as a court reporter while writing short stories under the pen name of Bog. The stories became very popular, and he published a two-volume set at age twenty-four. He was not only an entertaining storyteller but a social reformer. He became the editor of a newspaper, *The Daily News*, and his editorials attacked the social evils of his day. His books such as *Oliver Twist*, *Nicholas Nickleby*, *David Copperfield* and *Little Dorritt* helped form public opinion against the abusive practices of debtors' laws, public almshouses, and child labor.

THOMAS ALVA EDISON (1847–1931)

Born in Milan, Ohio, he is perhaps the most creative and most prolific of all inventors. His mother was a schoolteacher and worked hard to instill in him a love for reading. He began his career as a newsboy in the Grand Trunk Railroad when he was only twelve. In his spare time, he installed a laboratory for experiments in a baggage car and, acquiring a printing press, published the only newspaper ever printed aboard a train. At sixteen he became a telegrapher and bounced from job to job until, at twenty-one, he was considered a failure. However, he was independent, hardworking, and stubborn, and began looking for ways to improve the telegraph. One of his successful early inventions was the quadruplex method (four messages being received at the same time). As he gained backing, he expanded his thinking and soon invented the carbon telephone transmitter and the phonograph. His incandescent lamp was first demonstrated in 1879 when he was only thirty-two. Before his life ended, he held at least 1,300 United States patents. His creative inventions improved the lives of people everywhere.

LUDWIG VAN BEETHOVEN (1770–1827)

He was born in Bonn, Germany into a musical family: his grandfather directed the court orchestra and his father sang in the choir. However, the family lived in poverty because of his father's drinking. Beethoven developed a passion for the outdoors and, from an early age, felt that nature was the true source of music. His musical training began at age four; because he had obvious talent, he was often beaten in efforts to make him practice more. His first compositions were published in 1782 when he was only 12 years old. He studied with many of the world's masters, including Mozart, and, feeling restricted by his teachers' rules, began to create his own style. By the time he wrote his Third Symphony he was known as an original composer. In 1798 he began losing his hearing, and his Ninth Symphony, finished in 1823, was composed when he was completely deaf.

WALT DISNEY (1901–1966)

Born in Chicago, Illinois and raised partly in Kansas City and partly on a midwestern farm, he acquired some basic art instruction from correspondence courses, but dropped out of high school at age 17. He worked as a commercial illustrator, made primitive, animated, advertising cartoons, and tried to start his own business. When that failed in 1923, he moved to Hollywood where his older brother, Ray, helped him resume cartoon production. The invention of such cartoon characters as Mickey Mouse and Donald Duck, combined with a creative use of music, sound, and folk tales, made his Disney shorts a worldwide success. He expanded his dream, producing his first feature-length cartoon (Snow White) in 1938 and opening his fantasy theme park (Disneyland) in 1957.

PUT CREATIVITY INTO ACTION

- Practice something creative (drawing, painting, poetry, guitar) regularly for the whole month.

- Read a book that stretches your imagination.

- Look at a difficult situation or assignment you face from a different perspective.

- Join a community service project that offers a resourceful solution to a community concern.

- Try doing something that you've never done before, perhaps something you'd like to do but have felt incapable of doing well.

- Read a book about something you've always been curious about.

- Tackle a problem with someone you like and trust, and discover the rich resources of collaborative work.

- Write a letter to a local or national politician with a resourceful solution (or perspective) to an old problem.

COMMUNITY SERVICE IDEAS

- Make hand-decorated placemats or placecards and take them to a retirement home or hospital.

- Make birthday and/or holiday greeting cards for children with life-threatening diseases.

- Tell stories to children in a local hospital or to residents of a long-term adult care facility.

- Work with the elderly through a senior healthcare center.

- Volunteer with your local theatre company to help with an upcoming production.

- Make and display creative posters to spread messages of joy and happiness throughout your school.

- Think of a new and creative way for your class to contribute a unique service to the community.

BOOKS ON CREATIVITY

Butterfly Boy. Laurence Yep. New York: Farrar, Straus & Giroux, 1993.

Camille and the Sunflowers. Laurence Anholt. New York: Barron's, Hauppauge, 1994.

The Day of Ahmed's Secret. Heide and Gilliland. New York: Lothrop, Lee & Shepard Books, 1990.

Fox's Dream. Keizafuro Tejima. New York: Philomel Books, 1987.

Michael the Angel. Laura Fischetto. New York: Doubleday Books for Young Readers, 1993.

Rosie the Cool Cat. Piotr Wilkon. New York: Viking, 1991.

Is Your Bed Still There When You Close the Door? Jane M. Healy. New York: Doubleday, 1992.

"An Archeologist in Your Bedroom" – p. 138

"Can You Step in the Same River Twice?" – p. 171

"The Time Machine" – p. 130

"A Tour of Your School" – p. 132

"Why Do People Sing?" – p. 153

Character Education Year 2 Grades 6–12   **137**

Environmental Awareness

SUPPORTIVE VALUES

Beauty • Sacrifice

DEFINITIONS

Understanding that many factors determine the survival of an ecological community.

Becoming conscious of and making an effort to comprehend the complex factors which surround us and ultimately determine our survival is the key to **environmental awareness**. Making an effort to recycle, reduce, and reuse in our daily lives could be one example of an environmentally aware person. Caring for the land, loving the land, and understanding all it has to offer so that we can conserve and replenish it are also necessary aspects of this awareness.

A quality that gives pleasure to the senses or exalts the mind or spirit is **beauty**. Beauty as it pertains to our natural surroundings is our focus for this month's partner value.

Sacrifice is giving up something for an ideal or belief. The willingness to sacrifice self for the greater good of society is a trait which clearly defines a person of character.

PURPOSE

Making an effort to recycle, reduce, and reuse as part of one's daily life is a mark of an environmentally aware person. Understanding our environmental predicament and making our actions of conservation habitual will better equip educators to teach students the importance of these actions.

With our hearts and minds focused on the generations to come and our spirits centered on our obligation to the earth of which we are a part, we cannot help but become more committed to and more aware of the beauty of our environment. In recognizing and preserving the beauty of our earth we are leaving a gift of untold worth for generations to come. We must learn to honor the value of sacrifice, necessary for the survival of our planet, and realize that by giving up some of our conveniences we serve the greater good of all. The environment has taught us to understand that small sacrifices in the present can lead to great benefits in the future.

Environmental Awareness

Day One:
Use the definitions on page 139 as a springboard for discussing the meaning of environmental awareness.

Day Two:
There should be world-wide awareness of the need to protect the environment. Look at the list of words in other languages to gain a better understanding of the thoughts around the world that accompany environmental awareness (see page 141).

Day Three:
Work in small groups to consider the impact just one person has on pollution. List the ways in which you contribute to pollution. Do some research to find facts concerning how much waste/ trash a person creates each year, how much water a person uses, and how much food is wasted.

Day Four:
Make a list of ways people can reduce the amount of waste they contribute each year. Do you think you could take your own suggestions?

Day Five:
Why is it important to have clean water and conserve the water that we have? What can you do to protect the world's water supply?

Day Six:
Read some of Thoreau's poetry. Using Thoreau's poetry as an example, write a poem about nature.

Day Seven:
Select an endangered animal to do a one page report on. Include a picture of the animal in your report. Use completed reports for a classroom or school hallway display.

Day Eight:
Are any of these endangered animals within your region? If so, determine how you may alter your behavior to help these animals survive. If none of these animals live near you, choose one to adopt and find a way to help this species from a long distance.

Day Nine:
Using pictures from magazines or newspapers, create a collage to show wasteful uses of the earth's resources (for example, paper plates, aerosol cans, styrofoam, etc.).

Day Ten:
If your school does not recycle, make a plan for proposing a recycling project to your principal. Discuss ways in which students can be encouraged to recycle.

Day Eleven:
Do you know the difference between renewable resources and nonrenewable resources? If not, find out and make a list of each. Talk about ways to conserve our use of nonrenewable resources.

Day Twelve:
Choose a proverb bookmark from page 151. Decorate it and find a place at home or at school to use it!

Day Thirteen:
If possible, plant a tree in your school yard. If there is not enough money or enough space, make a small window garden and plant hardy wildflower seeds or small plants. Watch them grow.

Day Fourteen:
Do you know what a nocturnal animal is? If not, find out. Then write a short story about a nocturnal animal and what it does during a 24-hour period.

Day Fifteen:
Read a story about environmental awareness from the selection on pages 143–150.

Day Sixteen:
Plan and conduct a nature scavenger hunt. The list may include: ants, rocks, leaves, feathers, pine cones, dandelions, etc.

Day Seventeen:
Make a list of environmentally friendly classroom "rules" to hang up around the room (for example,
• "Don't waste water"—hang near the sink;
• "Recycle paper"—hang near the trash bin;
• "Turn the lights off"—hang near the light switch, etc.)

Day Eighteen:
Make a list of recommended environmental household "rules" to take home and share with your family.

Day Nineteen:
Study a micro-environment. With a partner, pick a grassy spot to place a hula hoop or circle made with rope or string. Get on your knees and write down what you see inside the circle (grass, clover, bugs, etc.).

Day Twenty:
Reflect on the lessons you have learned this month about environmental awareness and make a workable plan for embracing environmental awareness as a lifelong value.

ENVIRONMENTAL AWARENESS IN OTHER LANGUAGES

Chinese	*zi*	self, private, personal, natural
	ran	yes, certainly, really, still, nevertheless
French	*la conscience de l'environnement*	to be sensitive to and aware of one's relationship with one's surroundings and the external world
German	*umweltbewußtsein*	consciousness about the environment
Hawaiian	*malama 'aina* *aloha 'aina*	take care of the land love the land (malama means "to take care of, tend, attend, care for, preserve, protect, save, maintain" and 'aina means "land, earth," aloha means "love, affection")
Japanese	*kankyoo*	land without a border, surroundings; kan—"a round jewel that has even thickness, to go around, a circle" kyoo—"land border"
Latin	*conscientia de rerum natura*	environmental: from Old English en (in) + viron (circle); related to Latin vibrare (to vibrate) awareness: from Gothic "wars" (watchful) (watchfulness of that which is vibrant—alive—around you)
Spanish	*conciencia del medioambiente*	having a conscience about the environment
Tagalog	*kaalamang pangkapaligiran*	kaalamang: being aware and sensitive kapaligiran: the condition of all surrounding things

DISCUSSION QUESTIONS

- Do you think we are facing an environmental crisis?

- Do you think we have over-valued individualism and need to consider the needs of the entire planet?

- How often do you pause for a moment of meditation or prayer in response to the beauty of the earth?

- What concerns or worries you the most about the future?

- How does your family conserve water?

- Do you believe that everything in the world is interdependent and interconnected?

- Do you think humanity is inherently selfish and violent?

- What kind of earth do you hope your grandchildren will inherit?

- What aspect of the earth's beauty do you enjoy the most? What are you doing to insure its survival?

- What physical comfort would you sacrifice to preserve a healthy environment?

STORIES AND THOUGHTS FROM SPIRITUAL TRADITIONS

Hinduism

Know this my Prakriti
United with me:
The womb of all beings.
I am the birth of this cosmos:
Its dissolution also.
I am He who causes:
No other beside me.
Upon me, these worlds are held
Like pearls strung on a thread.

I am the essence of the waters,
The shining of the sun and the moon:
OM in all the Vedas,
The word that is God.
It is I who resound in the ether
And am potent in man.
I am the sacred smell of the earth,
The light of the fire,
Life of all lives,
Austerity of ascetics.

Know me, eternal seed
Of everything that grows:
The intelligence of those who understand,
The vigour of the active.
In the strong, I am strength
Unhindered by lust
And the objects of craving:
I am all that a man may desire
Without transgressing
The law of his nature.

— Bhagavad Gita

He is a true devotee who is firm in the thought, seeing the Lord in all creation, both what is and what is not.

— Ramcaritmanas

For the ignorant, the world is a web, in which to be tangled and strangled. To the wise, the world is God's creation and He is manifested everywhere within it.

— Tradition

Buddhism

The Buddha taught respect not only for human beings, but for all living creatures, near and far, large and small, visible and invisible. Respect for living beings includes respecting their habitats, refraining even from needlessly breaking the branches of trees, for they are the abode of countless beings. Awareness of our environment arises naturally when we reflect on the interrelatedness of all living beings. We depend on living beings for our food, our shelter, and our very life. We are all linked in a vast and complex web of interrelationships, where the welfare of one affects the welfare of the whole.

Let no harm come to living creatures, for each one values its life just as dearly as we do our own. Animals are not always as ordinary as they may seem, either.

The Golden Deer

Once upon a time in India, there was a very special golden deer named Suvarnapar_hva, who was the leader of all the many deer living in the forest. Not only was he as beautiful as silk and gems, he had the gift of human speech and the mind of highest enlightenment. One day while drinking at the bank of a river, he saw a hunter bound with rope and drowning, screaming for help. His friend the raven warned him away, saying, "Beware, this man is evil. He will commit the highest treachery." But Suvarnapar_hva, out of compassion, dived into the river to save him. Having been warned, though, he made the man pledge never to reveal the incident to anyone.

Meanwhile, Queen Moonlight saw this special deer in a dream and wished to see him in reality. The king, determined to fulfill the queen's heartfelt yearning, sent hunters out to capture the deer, but no one was able to sight him. Furious, the king offered a huge reward for the capture of the golden deer. By and by, the hunter who had almost drowned heard about the reward, and being evil and greedy by nature, went to see the king. He broke the promise he had made and betrayed the golden deer.

Soon after, Suvarnapar_hva's friend, the raven, spotted the soldiers of the king approaching with bows and arrows to capture the deer, and warned him from the tree tops. But the golden deer was unafraid. He said, "If they do not capture me, they will capture some other deer. This is my chance to protect others from harm."

Just then the evil hunter raised his bow to kill the golden deer. But as he did so, his hand fell off and dropped to the ground. Suvarnapar_hva went before the king and told him the story of how he had saved the hunter's life. The king was stunned when he heard the tale of the hunter's treachery. He invited the golden deer to stay in the palace, and prepared a jeweled throne for him. There, to the great delight of the people, Suvarnapar_hva taught the path of non-violence and respect for all living creatures.

Christianity

"O Lord our God, you have put people in charge of everything you made."

– Bible, Psalm 8:6

"And God saw everything that was made, and behold, it was very good."

– Bible, Genesis 1:31

Islam

"A gentleman takes as much trouble to discover what is right as lesser men take to discover what will pay."

– Confucius

These things have possessed the Tao from the beginning; Heaven, clear and shining; Earth, steady and easy; Spirits, mighty in magic; Vehicles, overflowing with joy; all that has life; and the rulers of men. All these derive their essence from the Tao. Without the Tao, Heaven would dissolve, Earth disrupt, Spirits All become impotent, Vehicles empty; living things would perish, and rulers lose their power.

– Tao Te Ching

How All Creatures Cry to God for Sustenance

> Yes, all the fish in the seas,
>
> And all feathered fowl in the air above,
>
> All elephants, wolves, and lions of the forest,
>
> All dragons and snakes, and even little ants,
>
> Yea, even air, water, earth, and fire,
>
> Draw their sustenance from Him, both winter and summer.
>
> Every moment this heaven cries to Him, saying,
>
> "O Lord, quit not Thy hold of me for a moment!
>
> The pillar of my being is Thy aid and protection;
>
> The whole is folded up in that right hand of Thine."
>
> And earth cries, "O keep me fixed and steadfast,
>
> Thou who hast placed me on the top of waters!"
>
> All of them are waiting and expecting His aid,
>
> All have learned of Him to represent their needs.
>
> Every prophet extols this prescription,
>
> "Seek ye help with patience and with prayer."
>
> Ho! seek aid of Him, not of another than Him
>
> Seek water in the ocean, not in a dried-up channel.

– Teachings of Rumi. The Masnavi p. 188
Book IV

[The purpose of this selection is to show that all forms of creation, not just humans, come from God. What God creates, therefore, is sacred and must be taken care of.]

Hawaii

Calabash of the Winds

The weather had been quite unpredictable and the demi-god, Maui, was feeling restless, so he decided to build a kite. He used a strong, lightweight wood for the frame and one of his mother's fine bark cloths, which was beautifully decorated, for the skin of the kite. He then lashed the skin and the frame together with long lengths of a strong bark which he twisted together for added strength. The kite was huge. When it was finished it was forty-five feet across and seventy-five feet long. The neighbors were amazed when they saw it, for none of them had ever seen such an enormous kite before.

There was not enough wind to fly it, so Maui and his friends carried the kite to find the Cave of the Winds, where the Keeper of the Winds lived. Along the way they passed men and women who were busy at work, pounding their bark cloth or planting taro; but when they saw the large kite they left their work and followed the boys to the cave.

Maui called out a greeting at the mouth of the cave and the Keeper of the Winds emerged from the darkness into the daylight to see Maui and his friends holding the kite.

"Dear Keeper of the Winds, could you call some winds so that I can fly my kite?" Maui asked.

The Keeper admired the kite, replying, "It is a fine kite; let's try it." He went inside the cave and returned with a small gourd which was covered by a lid. "This is the small gourd in which I hold the gentle winds."

They carried the kite to a large clearing and Maui chanted softly to the wind to come gently and lift his kite. The Keeper of the Winds slowly lifted the lid off the gourd and tipped it slightly to release a gentle wind. A light breeze lifted the huge kite a little way off the ground. Maui called for more wind and the Keeper uncovered the gourd a little further. The wind was stronger now, and lifted the kite so that it sailed over the trees. Maui let out more cord and called for more wind. His friends and the villagers shouted to the Keeper, "Give him more wind!"

The Keeper was as excited as the crowd, and he turned the gourd upside down as the magnificent kite climbed higher and higher and went out beyond the large, grassy clearing, beyond the tall green trees, and out over the turquoise ocean.

Soon the huge kite began to fall,so Maui and his friends quickly reeled it in and caught it as it came down.

The weather was beautiful the next day, so Maui and his friends carried the kite to the Keeper of the Winds again. "Today you must give me the winds from your large gourd."

"Those winds are not for kites; don't be a fool, Maui," cautioned the Keeper.

"But I am strong and my kite is magnificent," Maui retorted, and he began to chant for the mighty winds to come and fly his kite. The winds in the large gourd inside the cave began to tremble and moan. The Keeper ran inside and struggled to keep the lid on, but it popped off. The winds escaped from the cave and quickly lifted Maui's kite off the ground and shot it straight into the sky.

Maui laughed heartily, grabbed tightly onto the cord and planted his feet firmly on the ground. The winds were playing tug-of-war with Maui and his kite, and he was enjoying the battle of strength.

A cloud moved in and Maui could no longer see his great kite, so he called for the winds to return to the large gourd. But they were too far away to hear. Maui tried to reel in his kite. Suddenly he fell down; the cord had broken and he was left holding the stick which had been attached to the end of the kite cord. The winds had won the tug-of-war. They celebrated their victory, and soon a downpour chased everyone home.

The Keeper went into his cave and chanted for over an hour, trying to persuade the winds to return to their home in the large gourd, which they finally did. By the time the winds settled down, all the bark cloth which the women had set out to dry for the day had blown away, and the taro fields were all flooded.

Everyone in the village was very angry with Maui and would have nothing to do with him. The Keeper of the Winds was especially angry with him and would not answer his call when he went to the cave to visit. Maui became more restless with each passing day and finally decided to make another kite, which he flew near his home every day. As he flew the kite more and more he began to notice patterns in the wind, and slowly he came to understand the weather and which winds would bring rain and which would keep it clear.

One day, he saw a neighbor heading out to work in his taro patch and warned him about the approaching rain. The neighbor ignored him, but soon returned, soaking wet from the rain. Soon after, Maui saw another man going fishing, and cautioned him about a storm which Maui knew to be brewing. The fisherman paid no heed and was swept from the rocks where he was fishing and drowned.

After awhile, the villagers became aware of Maui's ability to predict the weather, and they began to rely on his knowledge. Would it be a good day to go fishing, to work in the taro patch, to take a sailing canoe to another island?

The attitude of the people toward Maui began to change, and he was respected for his special skill with his weather kite. They eventually forgave him for the storm brought on by his adventurous spirit, and honored him for his keen awareness of their environment, which enabled them to make safe decisions concerning their everyday work of survival.

Nigeria

Why the Sky is Far Away

Long, long ago the sky was not out of our reach as it is today. On the contrary, it was so close to the earth that people could reach out and touch it. Not only that, it tasted delicious, and if anyone was the least bit hungry all they had to do was reach up and grab hold of a bit of sky and eat it. It was wonderful! Sometimes it tasted like sweet potato, sometimes like roasted meat, or luscious fruit. There was so much of it! Indeed, a never-ending supply of delicious sky.

Because it was so easy to make a meal out of sky, there was very little work to be done. There were no crops to be sown or harvested. There was no cooking and thus no need to fetch water for boiling, or sticks for a fire.

Because there was so little work to do, people spent their time doing wonderful things like weaving beautiful cloth, or carving interesting objects, or telling tales, or making music. There were always exciting festivals to celebrate their happy lives. When festival time came there was a flurry of activity and preparation. The king of this happy land was called the Oba. In the Oba's palace there were servants whose only job it was to carve the sky into beautiful shapes for the festivities.

The sky, however, was growing angrier and angrier with the people. They had grown wasteful. They frequently took more than they could eat and then, without a care, threw the leftovers into the garbage. The heaps of leftover sky got larger and larger. Soon they were everywhere. There were chunks of half-eaten sky here, and barely nibbled bits of sky there.

"I'm tired of seeing myself wasted, strewn in pieces and piled in heaps all over the land," the sky said angrily. So one day, the sky turned very dark. Heavy, threatening clouds hung over the Oba's palace. Thunder rolled and lightning flashed right over the people's heads, and a great voice boomed "Oba! Your people are wasting my great gifts.They take more of me than they can use and toss me carelessly on garbage heaps all over your land. You must warn them, Oba, they must stop being wasteful or the gifts will be taken away!"

The Oba, afraid of losing the delicious sky, quickly dispatched messengers to take the sky's warning to the people. They were told of the sky's anger and warned to take only as much as they could eat and no more. They must not reach for the sky unless they were truly hungry. The people took the warning very seriously, as they did not want to lose their precious sky. For quite awhile they were very careful. Then came the time for the greatest festival of the year, which lasted several days. There was to be music and dancing and feasting. During the first few days of the celebrations, the Oba feared that the people would forget the sky's warning. He took care to make sure that no more sky was carved for the celebration than could be eaten.

Indeed, people continued to heed the sky's warning, but there was a woman in this land who was never satisfied. Whatever she had, it was never enough. She always wanted more jewelry, more children, more food. It was hard for her to obey the Oba's ruling, for she truly loved to eat. On the very last night of the festivities, she and her husband ate and danced into the night.

When she finally returned home, she said to herself, "What a wonderful evening it was. I wish I could relive it all—the music, the dancing, the food!" She gazed up at the sky, and, recalling all the delicious flavors and desiring to taste them all again, she reached up and grabbed a huge chunk. After only a few bites she began to feel quite full and started to toss the remaining piece on the garbage heap. "Oh, no! I mustn't throw this away," she cried and ran to her husband. "Husband dear, you must help me finish this piece of sky!" she begged. Her husband, who was exhausted from all the merriment, could manage only one bite. The woman ran to wake her sleeping children. "Children, you must help me finish this piece of sky!" she implored. But the tired children could only nibble at the chunk. Finally, the woman decided that enough had been eaten away and surely throwing away just a small piece could not be that bad. With that, she tossed the half-eaten piece of sky into the garbage heap.

Suddenly, thunder rolled and lightning flashed and a mighty voice boomed from overhead.

"Oba!" it cried, "Your people have been careless once again. They do not treat me with respect. I will leave you now!" With that, the sky began to rise higher and higher, and it did not stop until it got to be right about where it is today.

From that day on, the people had to work for their food. They had to sow and harvest crops. They had to hunt in the forests. The sky looked down on them as they labored, hopeful that they would learn not to waste the precious gifts of nature.

PROVERBS AND MAXIMS

There is religion in everything around us, a calm and holy religion in the unbreathing things of nature, which man would do well to imitate.

— *Ruskin*

I am glad I shall never be young without wild country to be young in. Of what avail are forty freedoms without a blank spot on the map?

— *A. Leopold*

We need wilderness whether or not we ever set foot in it. We need a refuge even though we may never need to go there . . . We need the possibility of escape as surely as we need hope . . .

— *E. Abbey*

No sacrifice is worth the name unless it is a joy. Sacrifice and a long face go ill together.

— *Gandhi*

We travel together, passengers of a little spaceship, dependent on its vulnerable reserves of air and soil; all committed for our safety to its security and peace; preserved from annihilation by the care, and the work, and, I will say, the love we give our fragile craft.

— *A. Stevenson*

HEROES AND HEROINES

ANSEL ADAMS (1902–1984)

Born in San Francisco, California, he grew up in the dunes area by the Golden Gate Bridge and developed a love of nature partly by watching the Pacific surf and the low fog moving across the sky. The other reason for his interest came as a result of his being tutored at home and being left by himself a lot; he found himself more responsive to the wild environments than to urban life. His career began as a thirteen-year-old wandering through the 1915 Panama-Pacific Exposition with a Brownie box camera. The following spring he visited Yosemite National Park with his Brownie. "From that day in 1916 my life has been colored and modulated by the great earth gesture of the Sierra." He continued photographing Yosemite every year through the 1970s. Few people have worked as hard or as effectively to preserve the American wilderness. His photographs "articulated" the concept of wilderness values; he touched countless lives with the importance of preserving the remaining wilderness lands.

JOHNNY APPLESEED (1774–1845)

Born in Massachusetts as John Chapman, there is very little known of his early life. One account mentions that his father served with George Washington and that he grew up with many younger half-brothers and half-sisters. He was a solitary child and would go for long walks in the woods, where he studied the behavior of the animals and birds. When he was 18, he and his brother walked across New York state. The next account has him at 25 in the Ohio River Valley, where he began his life work: traveling through the new land reading the Bible to settlers and planting apple trees wherever he went. He did this for fifty years and earned the respect of Native Americans as a medicine man, because he also planted herbs, made healing poultices, and brewed soothing tea. There are also stories of his bravery, such as the time he risked his life to warn settlers of an impending attack by the Native Americans. The orchards he planted may have vanished, but his legend as a caretaker of the environment will last forever.

RACHEL LOUISE CARSON (1907–1964)

Born in Springdale, Pennsylvania, Rachel owed her love of nature to her mother, who taught her as a tiny child the beauty of and a love for nature. Her literary talent became apparent at age ten when she began contributing articles to the *St. Nicholas League*, a children's magazine. She enrolled in the Pennsylvania College for Women with the intention of making writing her career, but a course in biology changed her mind. She rediscovered her interest in science, eventually becoming a member of the zoology staff at the University of Maryland. Combining her scientific skills and her writing ability, she became well known for her books *Under the Sea Wind* (1941) and *The Sea Around Us* (1951). She became a significant figure in the environmental movement and is best known as the author of *Silent Spring*, a controversial study of pesticide misuse, and as a crusader in the struggle for conservation and ecological awareness.

THEODORE ROOSEVELT (1858–1919)

Born in New York City into an old New York Dutch family, he was afforded an excellent education and developed an intellectual curiosity and a love of literature and the arts. To overcome the ill health and physical weakness of his early childhood he became a dedicated proponent of physical culture through sports and outdoor living. He graduated from Harvard and entered law school, but an interest in politics kept him from the legal profession. He was elected governor of New York, then became the twenty-sixth president in 1901 when President McKinley was assassinated. He is listed under Environmental Awareness because of his many successful conservation policies. During his presidency more than 150,000,000 acres were designated as national forests, thus saving not only forests but mineral, coal lands, and waterpower sites. His strong policies and leadership led to the National Conservation Commission and the Reclamation Act of 1902.

BRIAN SCHATZ (1972–)

Born in Ann Arbor, Michigan, he moved with his parents to Honolulu when he was two years old. Brian is the founder of an organization called Youth for Environmental Service (YES). In 1987, Brian went to Sandy Beach at dawn to surf, and found it closed due to a sewage spill. This inspired him to get involved in community environmental protection. He found few opportunities for a young person, such as himself, to make a difference in his community. Through his college years at Pomona College, he began to develop an idea for a way to empower young people to directly address their communities' environmental problems. This idea became YES. Starting with one phone line, limited funding, and some support from the University of Hawaii, he built this organization. It has since grown to include six staff people as well as offices in Honolulu, Maui, Seattle, San Francisco, and Los Angeles. Brian's philosophy is that everyone, young or old, can do something about local problems. All they have to do is take action.

PAUL WATSON (1950–)

Born in Canada, he has become one of the most daring of the environmental activists. He is one of the founders of Greenpeace and the Sea Shepherd Conservation Society. The original Sea Shepherd was a deep water trawler that Watson commissioned as the champion of sea animals that were being hunted into extinction. He scuttled the ship rather than let it be taken over by pirates, and found a cod trawler that he converted into the Sea Shepherd II. Since 1978 he has disrupted government-sanctioned wolf hunts and seal hunts, invented the tactic of tree-spiking to save old-growth forest from lumber companies, rammed Japanese driftnet ships, and confronted Russian whalers on the high seas. He has been arrested, beaten up, pursued by helicopter gunships and nearly killed. He is controversial, complex, and has been denounced as a terrorist by some. However, there is no doubting his passionate defense of whales, seals, seabirds, dolphins, and almost every form of endangered marine species. Future generations will probably consider him a hero.

PUT ENVIRONMENTAL AWARENESS INTO ACTION

• Be responsible and creative with left-over food.

• Plant a tree in your community.

• Take shorter showers.

• Volunteer to pick up litter along your favorite beach.

• Use rechargeable batteries.

• Volunteer to start or help with a community garden.

• Volunteer to maintain local parks and wilderness areas.

• Buy living Christmas trees. Be sure to replant them carefully.

• Learn how your legislators vote and let them know your views.

• Educate yourself on global and third world issues.

COMMUNITY SERVICE IDEAS

• Take younger students to collect litter around campus; talking to them about the importance of caring for the land.

• Help with trail maintenance, stream cleaning, park clean-up, tree planting, or volunteer with YES, or another local environmental group.

• Organize a recycling program in your neighborhood.

• Plant a garden.

• Volunteer with your local Nature Center.

BOOKS ON ENVIRONMENTAL AWARENESS

Antarctica. Helen Cowcher. New York: Farrar, Straus & Giroux, 1990.

Desert Giant: The World of the Saguaro Cactus. Barbara Bash. Boston: Sierra Club Books, 1990.

Eagle. Judy Allen. Cambridge: Candlewick Press, 1994.

Empty Lot. Dale H. Fife. Boston: Sierra Club Books, 1991.

Farewell to Shady Glade. Bill Peet. Boston: Houghton, 1966.

The Great Kapok Tree: A Tale of the Amazon Rainforest. Lynne Cherry. San Diego: Harcourt Brace, Jovanovich, 1990.

Little House. Virginia L. Burton. Boston: Houghton Mifflin Co., 1942.

Miss Rumphius. Barbara Cooney. New York: Viking Press, 1982.

Our Vanishing Farm Animals: Saving America's Breeds. Catherine Paladino. Boston: Joy Street Books, 1991.

Salamander Room. Anne Mazer. New York: Knopf, 1991.

Tiger. Judy Allen. Cambridge: Candlewick Press, 1992.

Tigress. Helen Cowcher. New York: Farrar, Straus & Giroux, 1991.

Tree of Life: The World of the African Baobab. Barbara Bash. Boston: Sierra Club Books, 1990.

Whistling Thorns. Helen Cowcher. New York: Scholastic, 1993.

Why the Sky is Far Away: A Nigerian Folktale. Mary-Joan Gerson. Boston: Little, Brown, 1992.

Zoo. Anthony Browne. New York: Knopf, 1992.

A Call to Character. Colin Greer and Herbert Kohl, eds. New York: Harper Collins Publisher, 1995.
    "The Immense Journey" – p. 365
    "Miss Rumphis" – p. 375

Earth Prayers. Elizabeth Roberts and Elias Amidon, eds. San Francisco: Harper, 1991.
    "Bless Thee, O Lord . . ." – p. 225
    "Find the Good Road" – p. 86
    "I Swear the Earth . . . " – p. 99
    "To Live Content . . . " – p. 108

The Moral Compass. William J. Bennett, ed. New York: Simon and Schuster, 1995.
    "The Wonder Tree" – p. 746

Freedom

SUPPORTIVE VALUES

Social Justice • Equality

DEFINITIONS

Being free to make choices and determine actions.

The **freedom** to make our own choices and determine what action we will take in any given situation is the freedom to which we refer this month. This freedom can be our salvation or our nemesis if it is not combined with a full understanding of the values of respect and responsibility.

Treating all people fairly, regardless of race, religion, gender, or sexual preference, is the definition of **social justice**. Akin to this value is **equality**, which asks that we treat all people the same in terms of education, housing, and job opportunities regardless of differences.

PURPOSE

Kenneth Sollitt explains, "Freedom is the opportunity to make decisions. Character is the ability to make right decisions. It can be achieved only in a climate of freedom. For no one learns to make right decisions without being free to make wrong ones." This is the crux of *Character Education*. As paradoxical as it seems, the freedom which allows us to make wrong decisions is the freedom which also enables us to build character. Freedom to make mistakes is an idea that educators embrace, because we know that it is when we strive to understand and correct our mistakes that learning occurs. Giving students the freedom to make mistakes by reassuring them that "there are no mistakes, only lessons" is one of the greatest gifts educators can give.

"We hold these truths to be self-evident: that all [people] are created equal; that they are endowed by their Creator with certain unalienable rights; that among these are life, liberty, and the pursuit of happiness . . . " Thomas Jefferson and the framers of the Constitution made the values of freedom, justice, and equality an integral part of that document. It follows, as Roberta Williams reminds educators, that "When we look for possibilities and potential in every student, then nurture those qualities, all children become successful learners." In this way we will be encouraging a classroom atmosphere where freedom, equality, and social justice can flourish.

Freedom

Day One:
Use the definitions on page 157 as a springboard to discuss the meaning of freedom.

Day Two:
Can you imagine what it would be like not to have your freedom? As a group, list all of the things you could not do without your freedom.

Day Three:
Using the discussion questions on page 160, talk with your classmates about what you know of freedom.

Day Four:
Think of the people you have studied or read about who were enslaved? How do you think these people must have felt? Put yourself in their shoes and write a journal entry about how it feels to be enslaved.

Day Five:
Imagine you are a slave who has just been freed. Continue your journal entry from yesterday about how you feel today and what you will do with your new freedom.

Day Six:
Choose a proverb bookmark from page 165 to decorate. Use it in your journal to remind you of those who fought for your personal freedom.

Day Seven:
Democratic nations rest on the basic principle that each individual has certain inalienable rights. Find the historical document that outlines these rights in your country and list them.

Day Eight:
Unfortunately, there are people even today who do not have their freedom. Write a letter to your representative in Congress to remind him or her to keep the value of freedom at the forefront of their policy efforts with foreign nations.

Day Nine:
Name some of the benefits of living in a democracy. How do citizens of a democracy sometimes take these benefits for granted and fail to think about how their lives would be different if these freedoms were taken away from them?

Day Ten:
Find out the name and address of your congressional representative and mail the letter you wrote. Discuss the importance of all citizens in a democracy learning about the people running for Congress and of going to the polls and voting for the candidate of their choice once they reach voting age.

Day Eleven:
Read a story about freedom from the selection on pages 161–164.

Day Twelve:
Freedom of thought and expression is the root of change in society. List some changes that have occurred throughout history due to this type of freedom (civil rights, women's suffrage, rap music, movies, etc.).

Day Thirteen:
Is freedom worth fighting for? Why? How can people who are not free embrace peace as a personal value while fighting for their own freedom? Write an essay on your thoughts.

Day Fourteen:
Read about the heroes and heroines of freedom on pages 166–167.

Day Fifteen:
Spread the value of freedom by choosing a community service project from page 168.

Day Sixteen:
Plan your service project and check your plans to make sure you have complete freedom to carry them out.

Day Seventeen:
Put the class community project into action.

Day Eighteen:
Freedom is one of the greatest gifts a country can give to its citizens. Plan a party to celebrate your own personal freedom.

Day Nineteen:
The primary responsibility of the armed forces is to protect the freedom of the citizens of that country. Find the names and addresses of people who protect your freedom and write them a personal thank you note.

Day Twenty:
Reflect on what you have learned this month about freedom. Embrace your freedom to live a fulfilled and happy life.

FREEDOM IN OTHER LANGUAGES

Chinese	*zi*	self, private, personal, natural;
	you	cause, means, instrument, source, motive; from, by, by way of, through
French	*la liberté*	possibility of acting, thinking and expressing oneself according to one's own choices; state of mind of a person who is not dominated by fear, prejudices, pain, or embarrassment
German	*freiheit*	liberty, freedom, privilege, immunity
Hawaiian	*ku'oko'a*	independence, liberty, freedom (ku means "to stand" and 'oko'a means "different, separate, unrelated, another; whole; entirety")
Japanese	*jiyuu*	be oneself
Latin	*libertas*	from Gothic "freis" (free)
Spanish	*libertad*	liberty, freedom, independence
Tagalog	*kalayaan*	having independence; being free; liberty; having free use

DISCUSSION QUESTIONS

- What are the freedoms you enjoy the most? Are there any limitations on these freedoms?

- What responsibilities accompany freedom?

- How do you define social justice?

- Have you ever been made to feel unequal to someone? Why do people do that to others? How can the Golden Rule be applied?

- Which freedoms are most essential for happiness in your life? For the common good of your community?

- Where does complete freedom end? What things should be controlled by law?

- What kinds of injustice infringe upon the basic human rights of people around the world? In America?

- Where is equality an issue in school? In the community?

STORIES AND THOUGHTS FROM SPIRITUAL TRADITIONS

Hinduism

Action rightly renounced brings freedom:
Action rightly performed brings freedom:
Both are better
Than mere shunning of action.

When a man lacks lust and hatred,
His renunciation does not waver.
He neither longs for one thing
Nor loathes its opposite:
The chains of his delusion
Are soon cast off.

The yoga of action, say the ignorant,
Is different from the yoga of the knowledge of Brahman.

The wise see knowledge and action as one:
They see truly.
Take either path
And tread it to the end:
The end is the same.
There the followers of action
Meet the seekers after knowledge
In equal freedom.

It is hard to renounce action
Without following the yoga of action.
This yoga purifies
The man of meditation,
Bringing him soon to Brahman.

When the heart is made pure by that yoga,
When the body is obedient,
When the senses are mastered,
When man knows that his Atman
Is the Atman in all creatures,
Then let him act,
Untainted by action.

– Bhagavad Gita

External freedom is temporary, it is gone the moment we become attached to things in the world. Internal freedom is permanent, for then our only possession is God.

– Tradition

 ─────────────────────── UNDERSTANDING

Having requires holding. Holding creates attachment. Attachment causes bondage. To be truly free is to let go of all desires and find peace within.

— Tradition

Buddhism

The greatest freedom is freedom from the delusions of the mind. One who is free from hatred, desire, and ignorance is truly free.

A prisoner unaware of being in jail never tries to get free. Similarly, ignorant beings unaware of being trapped in the wheel of birth and death never try to get free. Like birds in a gilded cage, they become complacent in their bondage and never seek the liberation of nirvana.

The robe worn by Buddhist monks and nuns symbolizes freedom, freedom from the bondage of ordinary appearances and worldly pursuits. As Zen monastics dress, they repeat this verse:

> "Vast is the robe of liberation
> A formless field of benediction
> As I wear the Buddha's teaching,
> Saving all sentient beings."

Noble beings achieve freedom from five fears: fear of not getting food and clothing, fear of speaking before large groups, fear of death, fear of birth in the lower realms (hell, ghost, and animal realms), and fear of teaching the learned. Through spiritual practice, they achieve pure memory, discriminating wisdom, enthusiastic perseverance, joy, ecstasy, perfect concentration, and pure equanimity. In the pure state of equanimity, they are free from obstacles and physical pain. They have no difficulty even in giving away their own body.

Before becoming a fully enlightened Buddha, Shakyamuni practiced for many lifetimes as a bodhisattva. One day while walking in the forest, he came upon a starving tigress with four newborn cubs. The tigress was so weak with hunger that, out of desperation, she was about to eat her own cubs. Instantly, the bodhisattva decided to cut off the flesh of his own thigh and feed it to the tigress to save her from the serious bad karma of eating her own children. Motivated by love and compassion, he saved her life by giving her his own flesh and blood. To this day in Nepal, the site of his generosity is commemorated and known as Takmo Luchin, "Offering his Body to the Tigress."

Freedom from eight worldly factors is the mark of a truly spiritual person. One is detached from: happiness from getting what one likes, unhappiness at getting what one dislikes, happiness from worldly pleasures, unhappiness from worldly discomforts, happiness from being praised, unhappiness at being blamed, happiness at hearing pleasant sounds, unhappiness at hearing unpleasant sounds. Freedom from these eight world factors results in peace and equanimity.

Zen Buddhism

The Original Mind is like water which flows freely without stopping at one spot, whereas the Deluded Mind is like ice, with which one cannot even wash one's hands and face. By melting the ice to water, it will flow anywhere; one can then wash one's hands and feet or anything. In one word, the mind freezes on one spot, it is "stopping." By freezing, there will be no freedom of use. Ice cannot even wash the hands and feet. Melt the mind and let it flow through your whole being and use it at any particular place as needed.

Christianity

"Do not use your freedom as an opportunity for evil."

– Bible, Galatians 5:13

"The Lord sets the prisoners free; the Lord opens the eyes of the blind."

– Bible, Psalm 146:7-8

"And you will know the truth, and the truth will make you free."

– Bible, John 8:32

"But let justice roll down like waters, and righteousness like an everflowing stream."

– Bible, Amos 5:24

Islam

Why Freewill is Good for Man

God said, "do thou grant his earnest request,
Enlarge his faculty according to his freewill.
Freewill is as the salt to piety,
Otherwise heaven itself were matter of compulsion
In its revolutions reward and punishment were needless,
For 'tis freewill that has merit at the great reckoning.
If the whole world were framed to praise God,
There would be no merit in praising God.
Place a sword in his hand and remove his impotence,
To see if he turns out a warrior or a robber.
Because freewill is that wherewith 'we honour Adam,'
Half the swarm become bees and half wasps.
The faithful yield honeycombs like bees,
The infidels yield store of poison like wasps.
For the faithful feed on choice herbs,
So that, like bees, their chyle yields life-giving food,
Whilst infidels feed on filth and garbage,

Character Education Year 2 Grades 6–12

And generate poison according to their food."
Men inspired of God are the fountain of life;
Men of delusions are a synonym for death.
In the world the praise "Well done, faithful servant!"
Is given to freewill which is used with prudence.

If all dissolute men were shut up in prison,
They would all be temperate and devout and pious.
When power of choice is absent actions are worthless;
But beware lest death snatch away your capital!
Your power of choice is a capital yielding profit,
Remember well the day of final account! *— Teachings of Rumi p. 152-3*
Book III Story XVI

Let there be no compulsion in religion. Truth stands out clear from error . . .
— Jonah (Yunus) 10:99

If it had been your Lord's Will, they would all have believed—all who are on earth. Will you then compel mankind against their will to believe?

The free will Allah has given us is the free will to worship as we please. It is to Allah alone that we must account for our choice. Men and women of Faith must endeavour to persuade the Faithless to submit to Allah, but we do not have Allah's permission to force anyone against his or her will to believe. Indeed, it is a contradiction in terms. If He had willed it, Allah would have created us without free will, but the merit of Faith is that it is arrived at through the individual's efforts and use of the abilities Allah has given to him to see the Truth. Faith imposed by physical fear, social or financial pressure is not Faith but hypocrisy . . . , for which both the false convert and his converter are guilty.
— Selections from Mishkat-ul-masabi [247] p. 160
The Cow (Baqara) 2:256

Chinese

"One who is free to choose, yet does not prefer to dwell among the Good—how can he be accorded the name of wise?" *— Confucius*

"You may rob the Three Armies of their commander-in-chief, but you cannot deprive the humblest peasant of his opinion." *— Confucius*

"One may govern a state by restriction; weapons may be used with skill and cunning; but one acquires true command only by freedom, given and taken." *— Lao Tzu*

PROVERBS AND MAXIMS

But what is liberty without wisdom and without virtue? It is the greatest of all possible evils; for it is folly, vice, and madness, without tuition or restraint.

— *Burke*

You can't hold a man down
without staying down with him.

— *B. T. Washington*

Whether women are better than men I cannot say—but I can say they are certainly no worse.

— *G. Meir*

Eternal vigilance is the price of liberty.

— *T. Jefferson*

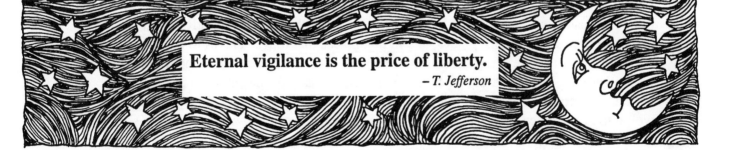

Freedom is the opportunity to make decisions. Character is the ability to make right decisions. It can be achieved only in a climate of freedom. For no one learns to make right decisions without being free to make wrong ones.

— *K. Sollitt*

HEROES AND HEROINES

BADSHAH KHAN (1890–1984)

Born as Abdul Ghaffar Khan, in the village of Utmanzai in the northwest tip of British India, he grew up on his father's farm in the shadow of the Khyber Pass. It was a time of unrest and calls for rebellion against the British rule. When Ghaffar was seven years old, the Frontier War broke out. He never forgot the suffering of his people and the way their strong spirit faded from their eyes. He heard the constant talk of hatred and fear. He grew up admiring the qualities of soldiers and also admiring the views of the headmaster of the mission high school in Peshawar, the Rev. Mr. E.F.E. Wigram. He was torn between going to the university and becoming a professional soldier. Several experiences led him to an Islamic school in Campbellpur and later to a mission school at Aligarh. By 1915 his strong presence and his dedication to India and to Islam earned him a reputation as a brave young reformer and, at age 25, he was proclaimed Badshah Khan, the King of Khans. But his method was different. From the most violent people in the world he created history's first non-violent army of over 100,000 men. He proved that strong people can be non-violent, and showed how violence has no place in Islam. Along with Gandhi he helped bring freedom to India.

HARRIET TUBMAN (1821–1913)

She was born a slave in the small village of Bucktown in Dorchester County, Maryland. Early in life she witnessed the injustice and terrible inhumanity of slavery. She endured many beatings and many long hours of hard labor, and developed a rebellious nature. She was seriously injured when she tried to help a slave escape; she was near death for months and never completely recovered. In 1849, no longer able to endure slavery, she simply left for the north one night with two of her brothers. Her brothers turned back, but she continued to Pennsylvania, where she quickly became involved in the Underground Railroad, an elaborate network of routes, guides, and hiding places that moved slaves to freedom in the north. She became one of the most active "conductors," and earned the name Moses. In spite of a reward of $40,000 for her capture, she helped at least 300 slaves reach freedom. She worked as a cook and a spy during the Civil War and continued working for human rights well into her eighties, appearing on the same platform as Susan B. Anthony. When she finally received a government pension, she used the money to find homes for the needy; she was still serving others when she died at age 93.

MARTIN LUTHER KING, JR. (1929–1968)

Born in Atlanta, Georgia, he attended the Atlanta public schools and graduated from Morehouse College in 1948. He was educated for the ministry at Crozer Theological Seminary and was ordained into the National Baptist Church. He received a doctorate in theology from Boston University in 1955 and it was while he was in Boston that he met and married Coretta Scott. While serving a church in Montgomery, Alabama, he became active in the National Association for the Advancement of Colored People (NAACP) and the Alabama Council on Human Relations. In 1955, when Rosa Parks was arrested for violating a segregated seating ordinance on a public bus, King and Ralph Abernathy, a fellow minister, organized a bus boycott. The boycott ended in triumph for black dignity, and King became a national hero. Organizing "Freedom Riders," voter registrations, lunch counter sit-ins, freedom walks and rallies for civil rights modeled after the non-violent protests of Gandhi, King became one the most important black leaders of his era. He was assassinated on April 4, 1968, while standing on a hotel balcony in Memphis, Tennessee.

NELSON ROLIHLAHLA MANDELA (1918–)

Born in Transkei, South Africa, he was the son of a chief of the Xhosa. Gifted with a strong will and a quick mind, he decided to fight the oppressive system of apartheid through the practice of law. He studied law at Witwatersrand University and set up his law practice in Johannesburg in 1952. He had joined the African National Congress (ANC) in 1944 and was already committed to a non-violent approach to dismantling apartheid. He was elected president of the ANC in 1951 and this marked the beginning of real turbulence in his life. He spent a total of twenty-seven years in prison, mostly on charges of high treason (apartheid perception of wanting equality, freedom, and dignity for the blacks of South Africa). Even in prison he continued to inspire those still involved in the struggle, and when he was released in February 1990 he received a tumultuous welcome wherever he went. He is the most significant political prisoner of the 20th Century and the most important reformer in South Africa. His life has become a symbol of human rights. He became the first president of a black majority-ruled South Africa and was awarded the Nobel Peace Prize in 1993.

SUN YAT-SEN (1866–1925)

Born into a peasant household in Choyhung in Kwangtung, China, near the Portuguese colony of Macao, he was established by his birthplace as a man of two worlds, China and the West. After a few years in a village school he was sent to Hawaii to join his elder brother. He enrolled in Iolani School, an Episcopal college preparatory school, where he focused on a study of science and religion. He graduated in 1882 and returned to his village in China. He spent his formative years in Hong Kong and, after beginning his medical studies in Canton, returned to Hong Kong, where he graduated from medicine in 1892. He became more interested in politics and was appalled by the Manchu government's corruption, inefficiency, and inability to defend itself against foreign aggressors. He became the preeminent leader of China's republican revolution and was instrumental in the overthrow of the Manchu dynasty in 1911 and the eventual reunification of the country.

PUT FREEDOM INTO ACTION

- Make good choices about watching TV and reading.

- Think about the way your language might be affecting others.

- Set an example as a "good sport" to someone who is younger.

- Always "play fair" in games and in relationships.

- Practice the Golden Rule.

- Make good choices about the way you treat others.

- Support the right of someone to disagree with you.

- Write a letter to the editor about human rights.

- Speak up when you see someone treated unfairly.

- Question authority wisely and politely.

COMMUNITY SERVICE IDEAS

- Write letters for Amnesty International.

- Volunteer at the local zoo.

- Volunteer with the Humane Society or another animal shelter.

- Tutor younger or second-language students.

- Volunteer to babysit or help to entertain children while their parents attend educational or community outreach programs.

BOOKS ON FREEDOM

All the Lights in the Night. Arthur A. Levine. New York: Tambourine Books, 1991.

To Be a Slave. Julius Lester. New York: Dial Press, 1968.

Follow the Drinking Gourd. Bernadine Connelly. Lincoln: GPN, 1993.

Journey of Meng: A Chinese Legend. Doreen Rappaport. New York: Dial Books for Young Readers, 1991.

Molly's Pilgrim. Barbara Cohen. New York: Lothrop, Lee & Shepard Books, 1983.

Nettie's Trip South. Ann Turner. New York: MacMillan, 1987.

The Red Comb. Fernando Pico. Mahwan: Bridgewater Books, 1994.

Seminole Diary: Remembrances of a Slave. Dolores Johnson. New York: MacMillan, 1994.

Sweet Clara and the Freedom Quilt. Deborah Harris. New York: Knopf, 1993.

Zoo. Anthony Browne. New York: Knopf, 1992.

RESOURCES FOR THE CLASSROOM

The Book of Virtues. William J. Bennett ed. New York: Simon and Schuster, 1993.

A Call to Character. Colin Greer and Herbert Kohl, eds. New York: Harper Collins Publishers, 1995.

Chicken Soup for the Soul. Jack Canfield and Mark Victor Hansen. New York: Guideposts, 1993.

Chicken Soup for the Teenage Soul. Jack Canfield, et al. Deerfield Beach: Health Communications, Inc., 1997.

A 2nd Helping of Chicken Soup for the Soul. Jack Canfield and Mark Victor Hansen. New York: Guideposts, 1995.

A 3rd Serving of Chicken Soup for the Soul. Jack Canfield and Mark Victor Hansen. New York: Guideposts, 1996.

A 4th Course of Chicken Soup for the Soul. Jack Canfield, et al. New York: Guideposts, 1997.

A 5th Portion of Chicken Soup for the Soul. Jack Canfield and Mark Victor Hansen. New York: Guideposts, 1996.

The Moral Compass. William J. Bennett ed. New York: Simon and Schuster, 1995.

Is Your Bed Still There When You Close the Door? Jane M. Healy. New York: Doubleday, 1992.

GENERAL RESOURCES

Books to Build On—A Grade-by-Grade Resource Guide for Parents and Teachers. John Holdren and E.D. Hirsch, Jr., eds. New York: Delta, 1996.

Educating for Character: How our schools can teach respect and responsibility. Thomas Lickona. New York: Bantam, 1991.

The Fifth Discipline. Peter M. Senge. New York: Doubleday, 1990.

Greater Expectations: Overcoming the culture of indulgence in America's homes and schools. William Damon. New York: Free Press, 1995.

How Good People Make Tough Choices. Rushworth M. Kidder. New York: Morrow, 1994.

Positive Discipline. Jane Nelson. New York: Ballantine Books, 1987.

Reclaiming Our Schools: A Handbook on Teaching Character, Academics, and Discipline. 2nd ed. Edward A. Wynne and Kevin Ryan. New Jersey: Prentice-Hall, 1996.

HEROES IN BOOKS

The Great Kapok Tree: A Tale of the Amazon Rainforest. Lynne Cherry. San Diego: Harcourt Brace, Jovanovich, 1990.

Beethoven Lives Upstairs. Barbara Nichol. New York: Orchard Books, 1994.

Lives of the Musicians. Kathleen Krull. San Diego: Harcourt Brace, Jovanovich, 1992.

Galileo. Leonard Everett Fisher. New York: Macmillan Publishing Company, 1992.

Shaka, King of the Zulu. Diane Stanley. New York: Morrow Junior Books, 1988.

The Great Alexander the Great. Joe Lasker. New York: Viking Press, 1983.

Theseus and the Minotaur. C. J. Naden. Mahwah: Troll Associates, 1981.

Perseus and Medusa. C. J. Naden. Mahwah: Troll Associates, 1981.

The Voyage of Osiris: a myth of ancient Egypt. Gerald McDermott. New York: Windmill Books, 1977.

The Sword in the Stone. Hudson Talbott. New York: Books of Wonder, 1991.

Johnny Appleseed: a tall tale. Steven Kellogg. New York: Morrow Junior Books, 1988.

Wolferl: the first six years in the life of Wolfgang Amadeus Mozart. Lisl Weil. New York: Holiday House, 1991.

Paul Bunyan, A Tall Tale. Steven Kellogg. New York: W. Morrow, 1984.

Go Free or Die: a story about Harriet Tubman. Jerry Ferris. Minneapolis: Carolrhoda Books, 1988.

What's the Big Idea Ben Franklin? Jean Fritz. New York: Coward, McCann, Geoghegan, 1976.

Honest Abe. Edith Kunhardt. New York: Greenwillow Books, 1993.

Gilgamesh the King. Ludmila Zeman. Montreal: Tundra Books, 1992.

The Trojan Horse. Warwick Hutton. New York: Margaret K. McElderry Books, 1992.

Mother Teresa, sister to the poor. Patricia Giff. New York: Viking Kestrel, 1986.

Good Queen Bess. Diane Stanley. New York: Four Winds Press, 1990.

Jane Goodall. Eleanor Coerr. New York: Putnam, 1976.

OTHER RESOURCES

Against Borders:
> *Promoting Books for a Multicultural World.* Hazel Rochman. Chicago: American Library Association, 1993.

The Best Years of Their Lives:
> *A Resource Guide for Teenagers in Crisis.* Stephanie Zvirin. Chicago: American Library Association, 1992.
> > A selective, annotative bibliography of fiction and non-fiction self-help works for teenagers, arranged under the following topics:
> > | | |
> > |---|---|
> > | *Family matters* | *School daze* |
> > | *Me, myself, and I* | *Crack, glue, or a six-pack or two?* |
> > | *Private property: don't touch* | *Wellness* |
> > | *Sex stuff* | *One plus one makes three* |
> > | *Death: romance and reality* | |

What Would We Do Without You?
> *A Guide to Volunteer Activities for Kids.* Kathy Henderson. White Hall: Betterway Publications, 1990.

Brothers, A Hebrew Legend.
> Florence Freedman. New York: Harper & Row, 1985.
> > This tale of brotherly love exemplifies the values of responsibility, compassion, generosity, commitment, sharing, and family.

Fables.
> Tana Reiff. Syracuse: New Readers Press, 1991.

When I Grew Up Long Ago:
> *family living, going to school, games and parties, cure and death, a comet, falling in love, and other things I remember.* Alvin Shwartz. Philadelphia: Lippincott, 1978.
> > Values from the "good old days."

The Newbery Award Reader:
> *A Collection of Short Fiction by Writers Who Have Won the John Newbery Medal.* Charles G. Waugh and Martin H. Greenberg, eds. San Diego: Harcourt Brace, Jovanovich, 1984.

BIBLIOGRAPHY

Resources for Buddhism

Tokunaga, Keiko, Graduate Student in Zen Buddhism, University of Hawaii, Honolulu, Hawaii.
Tsomo, Karma Lekshe, Philosophy Department, University of Hawaii, Honolulu, Hawaii.

Resources for Chinese Religions

Hsuan, Ko, (Aleister Crowley). *Tao Te Ching*. Maine: Samuel Weiser, Inc., 1995.
Ware, James R. *The Sayings of Confucius*. New York: Mentor Books, 1955.

Resources for Christianity

The Living Bible. Illinois: Tyndale House Publishers, 1971.

Resources for Hawaiian Stories

Alameida, Roy. *Stories of Old Hawaii*. Honolulu: Bess Press, 1997.
Kawaharada, Dennis. *Hawaiian Fishing Legends*. Honolulu: Kalamaka Press, 1992.
Pukui, Mary Kawena. *Folktales of Hawaii*. Honolulu: Bishop Museum Press, 1995.
Pukui, Mary Kawena. *'Olelo No'eau*. Honolulu: Bishop Museum Press, 1983.
Pukui, Mary Kawena. *The Water of Kane*. Honolulu: Kamehameha Schools Press, 1951.
Thompson, Vivian L. *Hawaiian Myths of Earth Sea and Sky*. New York: Holiday, 1996.

Resources for Hinduism

Bhagavad Gita. Trans. Prabhavananda, Swami, and Christopher Isherwood.
   New York: Mentor Books, 1944.
The Upanishads. Trans. Prabhavananda, Swami, and Frederick Manchester.
   New York: Mentor Books, 1948.

Resources for Stories from India

Ayier, V.A.K., *Stories of Vikramaditya*. Bombay: Dharatyia Vidya Bhavan, 1974.
Chandamama, Chandamama Publications: Vadapalani, Madras, India, December 1989,
   March 1994, April 1994.
Lao, Chaman. *Spiritual Stories of India*. Delhi: Publications Division, Ministry of Information &
   Broadcasting, Government of India.
Vivekananda, Swami. *Stories for Children*. Calcutta: Advaita Ashrama, 1994.

Resources for Islam

Rumi, Jalal ad-Din. *Discourses of Rumi*. Trans. A.J. Arberry. Great Britain: Curzon Press, 1993.
Brown, Kerry and Martin Palmer. *The Essential Teachings of Islam*. London: Century
   Hutchinson Ltd., ed. 1987.

Darbanid, Afkham and Dick Davis, translators of Farid ud-Din Attar's work, *The Conference of the Birds*. New York: Penguin Books Ltd., 1984.

Fazl, Mirza Abu'l, ed. and translator, Selections from Mishkat-ul-Masabih, *Chowk Minar Anarkali Lahore*. Pakistan: Sind Sagar Academy, 1977.

The Effendi and the Pregnant Pot. Trans. Primerose Gigliesi and Robert C. Friend. Beijing: New World Press, 1982.

Khan, Maulana Wahiduddin. *God-oriented Life: In the Light of Sayings and Deeds of the Prophet Muhammad and his Companions*. New Delhi: Islamic Centre, 1992.

Nizam ad-Din Awliya: Morals for the Heart. Trans. Bruce B. Lawrence. New York: Paulist Press, 1992.

Rumi, Jalal ad-Din. Trans. Reynold A. Nicholson. *Rumi: Poet and Mystic*. London: George Allen and Unwin Ltd.,1968.

Rumi, Jalal ad-Din. Trans. E.H. Whinfield. *Teachings of Rumi: The Masnavi of Maulana Jalalu-'d-Din Muhammad I Rumi*. New York: E.P. Dutton & Co., Inc., 1975.

Yusaf, Ali Abdullah. *The Meaning of the Holy Qur'an*. Brentwood, Maryland: Amana Corporation, 1992.

Resources for Judaism

Buber, Martin. *Tales of the Hasidi*. New York: Schocken Books, 1975.

Fahs, Sophia Lyon and Alice Cobb. *Old Tales for a New Day*. New York: Prometheus Books, 1992.

Schwartz, Howard. *Gabriel's Palace, retold*. Oxford: Oxford University Press, 1993.

Resources for Stories from Other Cultures

Compton, Patricia A. *The Terrible Eek*. New York: Simon and Schuster, 1991.

Demi. *The Empty Pot*. New York: H. Holt, 1990.

Freedman, Florence. *Brothers: A Hebrew Legend*. New York: Harper and Row, 1985.

Gerson, Mary-Joan. *Why the Sky is Far Away*. New York: Harcourt Brace, Jovanovich, 1974.

Goble, Paul. *Love Flute*. New York: Maxwell MacMillan International, 1992.

Han, Carolyn. *Tales from Within the Cloud*. Honolulu: University of Hawaii Press, 1997.

Heady, Eleanor B. *Jambo, Sungura*. New York: W.W. Norton and Co., 1965.

Kendall, Carol and Yao-wen Li. *Sweet and Sour Tales from China*. New York: The Seabury Press, 1979.

McDermott, Gerald. *The Stonecutter*. New York: Viking Press, 1975.

Polacco, Patricia. *Appelamando's Dreams*. New York: Philomel Books, 1991.

Rosen, Michael. *Crow and Hawk*. San Diego: Harcourt Brace, 1995.

San Souci, Robert D. *The Faithful Friend*. New York: Simon and Schuster, 1995.

Sierra, Judy. *Wiley and the Hairy Man*. New York: Dutton Children's Books, 1996.

Uchida, Yoshiko. *The Wise Old Woman*. New York: Maxwell MacMillan International, 1994.

Waite, Michael P. *Jojofu*. New York: Lothrop, Lee and Shepard Books, 1996.